COUNTRIES OF THE WORLD

Thailand

Gareth Stevens Publishing
A WORLD ALMANAC EDUCATION GROUP COMPANY

About the Author: A native of the United States, Ronald Cherry lived for three years on the island of Borneo doing rain forest conservation work. He has conducted forest research in Sri Lanka and studied anthropology in Chiang Mai, Thailand. He speaks Indonesian and Thai.

Written by
RONALD CHERRY

Edited by
CHRISTINE CHUA

Designed by
LYNN CHIN

Picture research by
SUSAN JANE MANUEL

This edition first published in 2000 by
Gareth Stevens Publishing
A World Almanac Education Group Company
1555 North RiverCenter Drive, Suite 201
Milwaukee, WI 53212 USA

For a free color catalog describing
Gareth Stevens' list of high-quality books
and multimedia programs, call
1-800-542-2595 (USA) or
1-800-461-9120 (CANADA).
Gareth Stevens Publishing's
Fax: (414) 225-0377.

© **TIMES MEDIA PRIVATE LIMITED 2000**
Originated and designed by
Times Editions
an imprint of Times Media Private Limited
Times Centre, 1 New Industrial Road
Singapore 536196
http://www.timesone.com.sg/te

Library of Congress Cataloging-in-Publication Data
available upon request from the publisher.
Fax: (414) 225-0377 for the attention of the
Publishing Records Department.

ISBN 0-8368-2327-3

Printed in Malaysia

1 2 3 4 5 6 7 8 9 04 03 02 01 00

PICTURE CREDITS
ANA Press Agency: 46, 47, 55, 58, 70
Archive Photos: 79, 80, 81, 82 (top)
BES Stock: 1, 2, 5, 7, 9 (top), 17, 26,
    27 (top), 34 (bottom), 38, 39, 42, 45,
    48, 61, 68 (bottom), 71 (bottom), 73,
    87, 91
Michele Burgess: 8, 14, 69
Blaine Harrington III: 4, 43, 84
The Hutchison Library: 3 (top), 20
John R. Jones: 33 (top), 71 (top)
Björn Klingwall: 53
Fiona Nichols/Times Editions: 15 (bottom)
Photobank Photolibrary/Singapore:
    3 (bottom), 6, 9 (bottom), 10, 12 (bottom),
    13, 15 (top), 16, 18, 19, 22, 30 (both), 31,
    33 (bottom), 40 (both), 44, 54, 57 (both),
    59, 60, 62, 63, 67, 78, 85, 89
Pietro Scozzari: Cover, 21, 32, 41,
    68 (top), 74
David Simson: 28, 72, 75
Eric Stein: 65
Still Pictures: 3 (center), 36, 50, 51
Liba Taylor: 23, 24, 34 (top), 35, 64
Vision Photo Agency/Hulton Getty: 76, 77
Nik Wheeler: 11, 12 (top), 25, 27 (bottom),
    29, 37, 49, 52, 56, 66, 82 (bottom), 83

Digital Scanning by Superskill Graphics Pte Ltd

Contents

AN OVERVIEW OF THAILAND

Welcome to the Kingdom of Thailand, the Land of Smiles! Except for the relaxed, gracious manners of the Thai people and the flavorful Thai cuisine, it is difficult to generalize about Thailand. Culturally, the country is diverse, with many ethnic groups and tribes. Although the modern nation is less than one hundred years old, the country has a long history of kingdoms that dates back over seven hundred years. Thailand has some of the most modern technology available, yet many Thai have traditional lifestyles. Although the economy depends heavily on agriculture, manufacturing and trade are increasingly important in the country's development.

Opposite: **Thailand's floating markets draw tourists, but they also serve the needs of the locals.**

Below: **Elephants share the road with vehicles in Surin, northeastern Thailand. Surin is home to the annual Elephant Roundup. This festival includes a feast for 200 elephants and a presentation of the animals' traditional roles in Thai battles and ceremonies.**

THE FLAG OF THAILAND

The flag of Thailand has gone through several changes. In the later half of the nineteenth century, the flag featured a white elephant, a symbol of the country and its monarchs, centered on a red background. In 1916, horizontal white stripes were added above and below the elephant. In 1917, the animal was removed from the flag, and a blue band was placed in the center. The flag of Thailand today symbolizes the three important forces of Thai life: the Thai nation, represented by the two stripes of red; the purity of the Buddhist faith, represented by the two stripes of white; and the monarchy, represented by the blue band across the center.

Geography

The Land

Thailand is often considered the heart of mainland Southeast Asia. It is the third largest country in the region, behind Indonesia and Myanmar. The total land area of the country is 198,115 square miles (513,118 square kilometers), approximately three-fourths the size of the state of Texas.

Geographical and climatic differences divide Thailand into four distinct regions: the central plain, the north, the northeast, and the south.

The central plain is the flat basin that surrounds the Chao Phraya River, which flows through the middle of the country from the northern highlands to the Gulf of Thailand. With a length of 219 miles (352 km), this river is the longest in Thailand. The Chao Phraya River and its tributaries provide irrigation for growing most of Thailand's rice, the main food in the Thai diet. The central plain area includes Bangkok, the capital city of Thailand.

THE MEKONG RIVER

The Mekong is one of the most biologically diverse river systems in the world, surpassed only by the Amazon and possibly the Nile. The river begins in China, passes through Laos, Thailand, Cambodia, and Vietnam, and ends in the South China Sea. Home to a wide array of aquatic life, the Mekong deposits mineral-rich silt on the flood plains of the Mekong Delta in Vietnam.

(A Closer Look, page 58)

The northern part of Thailand is known for its pleasant weather and beautiful hills and mountains. These mountains are the watershed of the Ping, Wang, Yom, and Nan rivers, which all flow into the Chao Phraya River. Doi Inthanon stands at 8,514 feet (2,595 meters) and is the highest point in Thailand. Chiang Mai is the main city in the north and the second largest city in Thailand. With its beautiful scenery and comfortable climate, Chiang Mai draws thousands of tourists each year.

To the northeast, the Phetchabun mountains separate undulating, sparsely forested terrain from the central plain. The Phanom Dangrek range extends eastward from the plain to the Mekong River, which forms Thailand's border with Cambodia and Laos. Northeastern Thailand, with its dry climate and sandy soil, is known for its difficult living conditions.

To the south, a long peninsula separates the Gulf of Thailand from the Andaman Sea. Thailand's tin mines and rubber plantations are concentrated in this region. The southern region has jungles, limestone cliffs, beaches, coral reefs just off the coast, and the last of Thailand's mangrove forests.

Above: **Coral reefs thrive in the crystal clear waters of the Phi Phi islands in southern Thailand.**

Opposite: **Thailand's elaborate network of canals, called** *khlong* **(klong), serves as a means of both transportation and irrigation.**

Left: **Known for their exquisite blossoms, orchids are, perhaps, Thailand's most famous flowers. Over 1,000 varieties of orchids are found in Thailand, many of which are cultivated for export.**

The Seasons

Thailand has a tropical climate, so the weather is warm throughout the year. The average daily temperature is between 75°–90° Fahrenheit (24°–32° Celsius).

In the central plain, the north, and the northeast, there are three seasons: the rainy season (June to November), the cool season (November to March), and the hot season (March to June). Changes in the climate depend on heavy seasonal winds known as monsoons. These winds blow in from the southwest during the rainy season and from the northeast during the cool and hot seasons.

The southern area is hot all year, and each coast has two seasons: rainy and dry. The dry season runs from May to October on the east coast and from November to April on the west coast.

THE GOLDEN TRIANGLE

Northern Thailand was a major producer of opium in the 1960s and 1970s. Opium was a source of income for the hill tribes. In recent years, the Thai authorities have been successful in providing the hill tribes with alternative crops, such as fruits, vegetables, and flowers.
(A Closer Look, page 52)

Plants and Animals

Thailand has many different ecosystems, ranging from rich marine life in the gulf to lush tropical rain forests inland. As recently as 1960, approximately two-thirds of the country was forested, although this figure has diminished to only about one-fifth today. Thailand's forests contain at least 15,000 different species of plants, 3,000 types of fungi, and 600 kinds of ferns.

The wildlife of Thailand includes elephants, tigers, leopards, rhinoceroses, bears, and monkeys. Thailand's rivers and coastlines are rich with aquatic life. Coral reefs on both the east and west coasts are home to several hundred types of coral. Marine life includes more than one hundred fish species and sea animals, such as the sea turtle, the dolphin, the whale, and the dugong.

Some plant and animal species have completely disappeared, mainly because of overhunting. For example, the Javan rhinoceros was hunted for its horn and is now extinct. Other species, such as the elephant, the tiger, and the dugong, are also in danger of becoming extinct.

The Thai government has established a network of national parks, wildlife sanctuaries, and other protected areas to provide safe habitats for wildlife. These protected areas cover over 13 percent of the country.

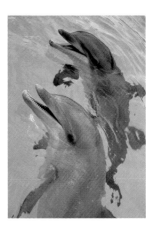

Above: **Dolphins live in the waters off the coast of Thailand.**

Left: **A leatherback turtle, a protected species, covers its nest with sand after laying as many as ninety eggs.**

SIAMESE CATS

A fourteenth-century book of Thai poems describes twenty-three types of Siamese cats. Today, only six breeds are left, including the famous Korat, or Si Sawat. Some people believe that Siamese cats bring good fortune and wealth to their owners. Giving a pair of Si Sawat cats to a bride is supposed to bring good luck to the marriage.

History

Prehistoric Times

Little is known about prehistoric cultures in Thailand. Archaeological excavations have begun only within the past few decades. The most famous archaeological site is near the northeastern town of Ban Chiang. Experts believe that early people living in this region cultivated rice and raised domesticated animals. Findings from Ban Chiang suggest that they knew how to make metal tools as early as 3500 B.C.

Early History

Thai are descendants of a race of people known as the Tai, who lived in China and began migrating south about one thousand years ago. Until the 800s, the area that is now Thailand was broken into small kingdoms and ruled by local lords. From the 800s to the 1200s, the neighboring Khmer empire of Angkor was the major power in Southeast Asia. This empire governed most of Siam, the name by which Thailand was known until 1939.

Left: **A mural painting depicts an early battle. Before the thirteenth century, Tai groups waged many wars against each other and foreign peoples.**

Rule by Thai Kings: Sukhothai to Ayutthaya

In 1238, a Tai lord named Sri Indraditya, and another Tai leader, Pha Muang, gathered an army and chased the Khmer rulers from the city of Sukhothai. Sri Indraditya then established the first Siamese kingdom. His son, King Ramkhamhaeng, expanded the kingdom to include parts of what is now northern Thailand, western Cambodia, eastern Myanmar, and Malaysia. By the late thirteenth century, the Tai people were calling themselves *Thai*. Sukhothai's glory lasted only as long as King Ramkhamhaeng's rule. After his death, the kingdom gradually declined in power. The kingdom of Ayutthaya took control of Sukhothai in the fourteenth century.

Ayutthaya was a powerful kingdom from 1351 to 1767. The Ayutthaya kingdom established diplomatic relations and maritime trade with countries around the world, including China, Japan, Portugal, the Netherlands, England, and France. However, in 1767, the neighboring kingdom of Burma (now Myanmar) invaded and destroyed the city of Ayutthaya. The Burmese took many prisoners back to their country, and their soldiers occupied the kingdom of Ayutthaya.

Above: **Wat Mahathat in Ayutthaya is a fine example of the kingdom's architecture.**

ARCHITECTURE

Thai architecture flourished during the Ayutthaya period, when some of the most magnificent temples were built. Most of Ayutthaya's buildings were destroyed by the Burmese, but the temple and palace ruins that remain tell of Ayutthaya's former glory.
(A Closer Look, page 44)

Left: King Bhumibol Adulyadej, Thailand's present monarch, and Queen Sirikit greet well-wishers at the king's birthday celebrations. Descended from the Chakri dynasty, King Bhumibol is also known as Rama IX.

RAMA I

Together with King Taksin, King Rama I (r. 1782–1809) played a key role in the struggle against the Burmese. Rama I (*below*) moved the court to Bangkok, the modern capital. He is credited with composing a new edition of the *Ramakian* to replace manuscripts that were destroyed when the Burmese attacked Ayutthaya.

A New Kingdom and a New Era

Soon after the Ayutthaya empire was destroyed, a Siamese official named Taksin, who had escaped capture during the attack, gathered a small Siamese army and chased the Burmese army back to Myanmar. The modern history of Siam begins in 1767 when Taksin was crowned king. He established a capital near what is now Bangkok. Under King Taksin's reign, the Siamese empire reclaimed areas conquered by the Burmese and conquered parts of the kingdoms of Cambodia and Laos.

In 1782, King Taksin became ill and was succeeded by one of his most successful generals, Chao Phraya Mahakasatsuk. After he was crowned king, General Chao Phraya was given the symbolic name *Rama*, after the hero in the epic poem the *Ramakian*. He was the first king of the current Chakri dynasty. His son was called Rama II, and all the kings since then have also taken the name Rama.

Surrounded by Colonies

During the nineteenth century, European explorers came to Southeast Asia looking for land and trade. Vietnam, Cambodia, and Laos became French colonies. Great Britain claimed Myanmar and Malaya (Malaysia and Singapore today) as British colonies.

King Mongkut (r. 1851–1868) and King Chulalongkorn (r. 1868–1910) skillfully encouraged Britain and France to keep Siam a neutral zone between their respective colonies. Siam lost some territory to each of these European powers but was never colonized. The Siamese kings' adaptability and diplomatic skills preserved Siam as the only free country in Southeast Asia.

Siam Enters the Twentieth Century

Chulalongkorn modernized the country by constructing railways, schools, and hospitals. Under King Vajiravudh (r. 1910–1925), Thailand participated in World War I on the side of the Allies. In 1932, under the reign of King Prajadhipok (r. 1925–35), a group of military officers staged a coup and forced the king to change the government from an absolute monarchy to a constitutional monarchy, thus reducing the governmental powers of the king.

LAND OF THE FREE

During the 1930s, a strong feeling of nationalism swept the country. The absolute monarchy ended, a constitution was written, and, in 1939, the government leaders changed the name of the country from Siam to Thailand, or *Prathet Thai* (prah-tet tie), which means "Land of the Free" in the Thai language.

Left: **A Siamese delegation visited the court of French king Louis XIV in the seventeenth century. A history of good relations with France and Great Britain helped Siam preserve its independence.**

World War II and After

In 1941, the Japanese army entered Thailand as part of Japan's campaign to control Asia. The Thai government decided to cooperate with the Japanese and declared war against the United States and Great Britain. There was resistance to this policy from a group called the Free Thai Movement. It opposed the Japanese and provided secret assistance to the Allied forces fighting the Japanese. Near the end of the war, the Free Thai Movement gained control of the country and fought openly against Japan.

In 1946, the young King Ananda Mahidol was killed only a few months after his coronation. His nineteen-year-old brother, Bhumibol Adulyadej, was crowned king. Thailand joined the United Nations that same year. The government in the postwar period consisted of the military and bureaucratic elite. Changes of government took place with bloodless coups. This period was followed by relative stability during the 1980s, and Thailand's economy expanded. However, the military remained a powerful force in Thai politics in the 1990s.

Above: This memorial is located at Kanchanaburi, near the bridge over Khwae Noi River (River Kwai) in Thailand. During World War II, thousands of Allied prisoners died under their Japanese captors while building this infamous bridge to Burma.

REFUGEES

Since 1975, when many neighboring countries became communist, more than one million refugees have fled to Thailand. While most refugees have been resettled, a large number remains in refugee camps near the border.

(A Closer Look, page 64)

King Ramkhamhaeng (r. 1279–1298)

Ramkhamhaeng, one of the first kings of the powerful kingdom at Sukhothai, was a brilliant politician and warrior. He created the Thai alphabet that is currently used today. During his reign, arts and literature flourished. A stone inscription from his reign is the earliest example of Thai literature. Thai schoolchildren today are required to learn the beginning of this inscription, which describes Ramkhamhaeng's reign as a time of peace and prosperity.

King Chulalongkorn (r. 1868–1910)

King Chulalongkorn (Rama V) is known for his contributions to Siam's modernization. During his time, people who owed money to others could be forced into slavery to pay their debts. Parents could sell their children, and husbands could sell their wives. Perhaps his most famous act was the abolition of slavery in 1905. He also abolished a law that required all people to crawl and bow before the king. He supported the construction of roads, railways, and hospitals. Thailand's first university was established in 1916 and named Chulalongkorn University in his honor.

King Chulalongkorn

Chan and Mook

Chan and Mook are famous for repelling a Burmese invasion in 1875. Chan was the widow of the governor of the southern city of Thalang on the island of Phuket; Mook was Chan's younger sister. When the Burmese launched a massive invasion along the Thai-Burmese border, there was no Thai army in the south to fight them. Chan and Mook organized a militia, collected weapons, directed the construction of fortresses from coconut trees, and developed a strategy to repel the invasion. The two women, dressed as male soldiers, led the Thalang militia into battle. The Burmese army had moved along the southern peninsula with little trouble until it met Chan and Mook and their soldiers at Thalang. They defeated the Burmese despite being greatly outnumbered. The two sisters were recognized as heroes by King Rama V, who gave them royal titles. Today, a statue of the two sisters brandishing swords stands on the island of Phuket, in tribute to their valor.

Chan and Mook

Government and the Economy

Levels of Government

Since 1932, the Thai government has been a constitutional monarchy. This means that the king has little power over the government and does not play an official role in governing the country.

The main governing body is the National Assembly, made up of the Senate and the House of Representatives. The prime minister, chosen from the members of the House of Representatives, is the head of the government. Each government department is headed by a minister.

The country is divided into seventy-six *changwat*, or provinces, each headed by a governor. The provinces are divided into *ampoe* (alm-per), or districts, run by district chiefs, who are appointed by the governors. Districts are divided into villages, each run by a headman elected by the villagers.

THE KING

The Thai constitution limits the king's role to that of ceremonial head of state. However, the king can dissolve the government and call for a new election or impose an immediate curfew if he feels the nation is threatened. The current king has never had to use these powers, but the fact that he has them probably encourages politicians to act in the best interests of the Thai people.
(*A Closer Look, page 56*)

Left: Soldiers lead a parade on Armed Forces Day in Chiang Mai. The military plays an active role in politics and social development as well as in the defense of the nation. Most of the political parties in Thailand are organized and run by former generals and admirals.

Opposite: The king presides over the opening of the National Assembly.

International Politics

Thailand has maintained good relations with other countries, particularly with the United States, the United Kingdom, and France. Thailand sent troops to fight with the United States in the Korean War, and later, in the Vietnam War.

In 1954, Thailand became the headquarters for the Southeast Asia Treaty Organization (SEATO), a group of Asian and Western nations working together for military cooperation.

In 1967, Thailand was a founding member of the Association of Southeast Asian Nations (ASEAN), set up to improve both economic and political relations among the leading non-communist countries of Southeast Asia. The other original members of ASEAN were Indonesia, Malaysia, the Philippines, and Singapore. Thailand helped improve relations between the ASEAN countries and other countries in the region, such as Myanmar, Vietnam, Cambodia, and Laos. During the 1990s, these countries also became members of ASEAN.

THE MILITARY

Since the creation of the constitutional monarchy in 1932, the Thai military has had an active role in the government and politics of Thailand. Between 1932 and 1976, the military took over the government ten times. Although the military still has strong influence today, this power is weakening.

Economy

Traditionally, agriculture and resource industries have been the most important sectors of the Thai economy. About 55 percent of the population works in agricultural jobs, and about 40 percent of Thailand's total land area is used for agriculture. Key crops include rice, rubber, and copra. Thailand not only produces enough rice for Thai people but also exports more rice than any other country in the world. Thailand is one of the largest rubber producers, controlling 33 percent of the world's total production. Ninety-five percent of the world's exports of tapioca, which is consumed by both humans and livestock, comes from Thailand.

Natural resources such as zinc and tin are mined in southern Thailand and play an important role in the Thai economy. In recent years, the manufacturing sector has grown, especially in textiles, computer components, and automobile parts. Tourism is one of the biggest industries in Thailand.

Above: **Along the coasts of Thailand, fishing is a primary source of income.**

DEFORESTATION

One of Thailand's natural resources is timber, especially, teak wood. Teak is used in building ship decks, houses, and furniture. However, intense logging has resulted in the destruction of Thailand's forests. Today, logging is banned in Thailand.
(A Closer Look, page 50)

Economic Growth and Downturn

Since the late 1970s, the economy of Thailand has grown rapidly. This means that the number and types of businesses have increased, creating job opportunities and wealth for Thai people. In the 1980s, many foreign businesses invested their money in Thai banks because of the strong economy. The banks then loaned money to Thai businesses that were increasing in size. More business also meant more government income from taxes. These taxes paid for improvements in the quality of education, health care, and public utilities. By the mid-1990s, the Thai economy was growing faster than many other Southeast Asian economies.

In July 1997, there was an economic downturn, and many Thai companies were not able to repay their bank loans. This meant that many foreign businesses no longer trusted the Thai banks, so they took their money out of Thailand. Suddenly, the economy became unstable, and the prices of goods and services increased drastically. Many people lost their jobs. Other countries, such as the United States and Japan, had to loan Thailand money so the government could provide food and assistance to the Thai people. By the end of 1999, the Thai economy was doing better, but it will take some years for the country to be as prosperous as it once was.

TOURISM

Tourism forms a large part of the Thai economy and generates many jobs. The Tourist Authority of Thailand is an important government department.
(A Closer Look, page 72)

Below: **The automobile components industry has benefited from Thailand's reasonable labor costs.**

People and Lifestyle

Ethnic Groups

There are about thirty ethnic groups living in Thailand, but all citizens of Thailand are called *Thai*, as this is their nationality. The various ethnic groups within Thailand identify themselves by race, culture, and language.

About forty-five million people, or 75 percent of Thailand's population, are ethnic Thai. Although they are concentrated in the broad central plain in the middle of the country, the ethnic Thai also live throughout the southern region, the northeastern region, and in the flat valleys of the north.

The largest minority group is the Chinese, often called *Chinese-Thai*. The first Chinese came to Thailand thousands of years ago as traders and ambassadors from China. Most of the Chinese-Thai now living in Thailand descend from Chinese immigrants who came to Thailand less than 200 years ago. Because these immigrants often arrived by boat, many

BANGKOK

The fastest way to beat Bangkok's infamous traffic jams is via the river in one of the many river taxi services.
(A Closer Look, page 46)

Below: **Religion plays a big part in the life of almost every Thai. For many Buddhists, the temple is the center of community life.**

Above: **The Lisu, originally from eastern Tibet, first arrived in Thailand in 1921.**

Chinese settled near the port in Bangkok. Even today, Bangkok has a special Chinatown area. Most Chinese-Thai live in cities, although some live in rural areas throughout the country. Many of them are merchants and traders, but some are farmers, too.

Another important minority is the Thai Malays in the south. They are more closely related to the Malay people of Malaysia than they are to the ethnic Thai. Thai Malays speak Malay and Thai and practice Islam. In the early 1980s, many Malays fought for separation from Thailand. They wanted to be part of Malaysia. There was considerable violence and terrorism, and government buildings were bombed. However, by the 1990s, the separation issue had died down, and the Malays have now accepted that they are Thai nationals.

The third important minority in Thailand is the hill tribes, who live in the mountains of the northern and northeastern regions. Over the last one hundred years, the hill tribe people have moved into northern Thailand from southern China and from the neighboring countries of Myanmar and Laos. There are now six major hill tribe groups.

HILL TRIBES

The hill tribes in Thailand include the Karen, Hmong, Yao, Lahu, Akha, and Lisu. Since the 1960s, government aid for these minority groups has included improved health and social services as well as agricultural assistance.
(A Closer Look, page 54)

Family Life

Thai families tend to be loosely structured, and it is common for a household to include several generations as well as cousins or other distant relatives. Sometimes non-relatives may be included in a family. They are called "aunt" or "uncle" by the rest of the family. Thus, to feel a part of the family, people do not have to be related; they just have to participate in and contribute to the family's life.

Respect for One's Elders

In Thai culture, young children are taught early to show respect for those older than themselves. For example, younger children cannot call their older siblings by their names; they must use the title "big brother" or "big sister." It is impolite not to use these titles. Using familiar titles such as "aunt," "uncle," or "big brother/big sister" is also required when speaking with older friends. This family-like feeling among unrelated people is found in both domestic and work settings throughout Thailand.

Above: **A nuclear family in Thailand is rare, as most people live in large extended families. This Thai family is on vacation at a local island resort.**

NICKNAMES

Thai people usually have just a first name and a family name. Since Thai names often consist of four or five syllables, children are given short one-syllable nicknames. Common nicknames for girls include Soam (orange) and Nit (little). Common boy's nicknames include Wute (weapon) and Wat (temple).

Wai

A very important part of Thai culture is the *wai* (why), a gesture used to show respect to those older or in positions of power. It is a slight bow of the head accompanied by pressing the palms of the hands together and raising them in front of the chin. Instead of shaking hands, Thai people wai when meeting or saying good-bye. Children wai to parents and grandparents. It is rude to forget to wai.

The Role of Women

Thai women play significant social and economic roles in Thai society, not only as mothers and household managers but also as workers and small business owners in Thailand's industrial sector. As Thailand becomes more modernized, many rural women are seeking new lives and employment in urban areas. The modernization and urbanization of lifestyles have caused tremendous changes in the structure of the traditional rural extended family.

BUDDHISM

Buddhism plays an important role in Thai family life. Monks bless wedding ceremonies, and funerals are held at temples. Temples are also home to the many Thai men who become Buddhist monks for a short while. On Buddhist holidays, families gather to decorate the neighborhood temple.
(A Closer Look, page 48)

Below: **In Thailand, it is never too young to start learning the wai.**

Education

The old traditional system of education in Thailand was based on the Thai philosophy of life. It emphasized Buddhism, respect for the king, and loyalty to family.

In 1887, King Chulalongkorn set up a department of education. He invited Western educators to be advisers, thus signaling the arrival of a modern public education system in Thailand.

Compulsory education began in 1921 and called for universal school attendance starting at age seven and continuing through to sixth grade. In 1960, the age for compulsory education was extended to fourteen. Public schools are free, but parents have to pay for school uniforms and supplies. Thai is the language of instruction at all levels, and English is taught as a second language after fourth grade.

Approximately 95 percent of the Thai population is literate. Nearly seven million children per year attend elementary school, but less than a million go on to high school, and even fewer go to college. Many young people face pressure to leave school and find jobs so they can help support their families.

Below: **Children in a village school work at their lessons.**

Higher Education

The first university, Chulalongkorn University, was founded in Bangkok in 1916. Today, there are more than thirty government and private universities. High school students must take a national examination, conducted twice annually, in October and March, to qualify for admission into the government universities. All graduating high school students take the test and are ranked according to their test scores. Students with high scores can opt to study medicine, law, or engineering at the university of their choice.

For many Thai, a university education is perceived as a means to a better life. Competition for entry into prestigious universities, such as Chulalongkorn University and Thammasat University, is intense. A few thousand students compete every year for only a few hundred places. This intense competition has given rise to a number of private tutoring schools, which prepare students for the difficult university admission tests.

Above: **Lunch break in school is a time for relaxation and laughter.**

Religion

Buddhism is the official religion of Thailand and is practiced by 95 percent of the population. Buddhist monks often lead prayers at official ceremonies or public gatherings. Some Buddhists strictly follow the rules and regularly go to the temple, whereas others may go to the temple only on special holidays.

In every Thai neighborhood or village, there is a *wat* (waht), or temple, where people can worship. They may pray and offer their respects to the Buddha in a general hall in the temple. A special sanctuary inside the temple contains a Buddha image.

Most Chinese in Thailand are Buddhists. However, they also practice ancestor worship and pray to gods from the Taoist tradition. Taoism is a philosophical and religious tradition that emphasizes simplicity in living and harmony with nature. Taoists seek a perfected state of immortality.

Thailand has a tradition of tolerance toward other religions. Muslim traders from the Middle East, India, Malaysia, and Indonesia brought Islam to southern Thailand centuries ago.

SPIRIT HOUSES, AMULETS, AND TATTOOS

In addition to following Buddhist precepts, the Thai believe that many spirits affect their daily lives. For protection from evil spirits, many Thai build spirit houses in their homes and offices and present regular offerings. They also believe that amulets and tattoos have the power to protect them from misfortune.
(A Closer Look, page 70)

Left: The Wat Phra Keo, in the Grand Palace, Bangkok, is home to the Emerald Buddha, which Thai people regard as the most important Buddhist image in the world.

Left: **Buddhists observe** *Wisaka Bucha* **(wee-sah-kah boo-chah), the most important Buddhist festival. Wisaka Bucha celebrates the Buddha's birth, the day of his enlightenment, and his death.**

Today, Muslims make up just under 4 percent of the Thai population and remain concentrated in the south. Some Muslim parents send their children to Islamic religious or vocational schools. Muslim children who attend Thai schools also receive weekly religious instruction in Islam.

About 0.5 percent of the Thai population is Christian. Christian churches are only found in larger cities, or in rural areas where there was a missionary presence. Despite converting only a relatively small number of people, Christian missionaries helped establish some of Thailand's first hospitals in the mid-1800s.

The hill tribes mostly practice animism, which is closely linked to their agricultural life. Animism is the worship of the spirits of nature. Animists believe that all things — the weather, the night, the sun, and even stones — have souls.

Less than 0.1 percent of the population is Hindu. Thai Hindus are primarily the descendants of traders from India who moved to Thailand.

Below: **Larger cities throughout the country have at least one mosque for their Muslim citizens.**

Language and Literature

Language

Thailand's national language is called Thai. Scholars believe that Thai is a form of Chinese that was gradually brought to the area between the seventh and thirteenth centuries. Within Thailand, there are actually several different Thai languages, but the one used by the government, schools, and the media is the language known as Central Thai. Central Thai was originally spoken by the people of Bangkok and the central plain. Having one official language enables people who otherwise use different ethnic languages to communicate with each other.

Opposite: A wide range of newspapers and magazines is published in the Thai language.

A TONAL LANGUAGE

Thai is a tonal language with five tones: high, middle, low, rising, and falling. Each syllable of a Thai word must be pronounced correctly and vocalized at a certain pitch. If the pitch is different, the word might have another meaning. For example, the word pronounced "my" can be said in four different tones, each producing a different meaning. "My" said in a high tone means "wood," and "my" said in a low tone means "new." These tonal differences make Thai a difficult language for foreigners to learn.

Left: Signs in the city streets are usually written in the Thai language. This sign reminds motorists to wear their safety belts. The banner (*upper right*) urges motorcyclists to wear helmets and asks all motorists to adhere strictly to traffic regulations.

Literature

King Ramkhamhaeng's *Inscription No. 1*, written in 1292 and describing the prosperity of the Sukhothai kingdom, is considered to be the first Thai literary work. King Ramkhamhaeng is also credited with producing the first Thai poem, *The Maxims of King Ruang*, which extols the values of goodness and virtue. The Ayutthaya period was a time when Thai classical literature, especially poetry, flourished.

Perhaps the most widely read Thai work is the *Ramakian* (rah-mah-kee-un), the Thai version of the classic Indian epic the *Ramayana*, which tells the story of the great king Rama. Another Thai classic is the epic poem *Phra Aphaimani*.

Novels have been an important part of Thai literature since the early 1900s. In the 1920s, Thai literature and journalism flourished. Novelists such as Kulap Saipradit, Dok Mai Sot, and Prince Akatdamkoen, have written about the conflicts between European and Asian values.

KUKRIT PRAMOJ

Kukrit Pramoj is a famous novelist and journalist who also served as Thailand's prime minister from 1975 to 1976. His novels comment on Thai life and politics. His most famous book is *The Four Reigns*, which tells the story of a noble family from the late 1800s to World War II. Another well-known work is *Red Bamboo*, which has an anti-communist message. Many of Kukrit Pramoj's works have been translated into English.

29

Arts

Thai Performing Arts

The arts of ballet and play-acting are combined in two forms of Thai theater: classical theater and traditional theater. Classical theater is an older art form that is known by most Thai but is rarely performed, and then only at a few theaters in the country. Traditional theater is more popular among the locals and is commonly performed throughout the country, in both cities and rural areas. Both classical and traditional theater are losing their appeal today, as Thai people increasingly prefer to watch movies and television.

Khon and Lakhon

The two common forms of classical theater are the *khon* (kohn) and the *lakhon* (lah-kohn). The khon has its roots in elaborate performances at the royal palace. The performance includes masked silent actors in intricate costumes who move on stage, following the words of a narrator or chorus. The performers move about the stage in quick leaps and slow turns. An orchestra of traditional instruments accompanies this performance.

Above: **In a khon performance, masked actors on stage are accompanied by narrators.**

Left: **Aspiring dancers undergo rigorous training at a dance school in Bangkok.**

SILK

Silk products are an important part of Thailand's tourism industry. The silk weavers are mostly women, who produce a range of silk products that includes everything from fabrics to blouses, scarves, bedcovers, and furnishings.
(*A Closer Look, page 68*)

The khon tells stories of mythical characters including kings, warriors, and demons. Perhaps the most popular stories are those from the *Ramakian*, which describe the adventures of King Rama.

The lakhon, another form of classical theater, was a favorite with common people. Lakhon performances are based on stories, including tales from the *Ramakian* as well as Thai folktales. Performers are not masked, and thus can talk onstage. The performance is less acrobatic than that of the khon. Instead, actors and actresses often keep their feet still so all the motion is in their upper bodies. Songs and music that help tell the story accompany the action onstage.

Likay

The *likay* (lee-kay), the most common form of traditional theater, is not delicate or complicated like classical theater. Instead, the likay is a comedy in which the performers are loud and emotional. Costumes are brightly colored and makeup is exaggerated. The actors and actresses often interact with the audience. Still performed at public festivals and rural county fairs, the likay remains popular in modern times, and likay performances are shown on television every day.

PUPPET THEATER

Traditional puppet performances are called nang yai and *nang talung* (nang tah-loong). The puppets are hidden from the audience behind a white screen and are lighted from behind. Thus, the audience can only see the puppets' shadows. These performances often tell stories from the *Ramakian*. Puppet theater used to be common throughout Thailand, but is now mainly performed in Thailand's southern provinces.

Thai Music

Classical Thai music is played by an orchestra of musicians using traditional Thai instruments. Traditionally, the classical musicians were part of a king or nobleman's court. Musicians developed their skills as apprentices in the court orchestra. The Thai orchestra was used to accompany all kinds of theater performance, as well as at social events.

Another kind of traditional Thai music is village folk music. Village folk music has existed for hundreds of years and continues to be a part of village festivals and temple ceremonies. The instruments are simple, and the songs are about the hardships of village life, the rice harvest, or love.

Today, rock, pop, and jazz music have become a part of Thai music. Both Thai and Western rock musicians have large followings and give sold-out concerts to audiences of screaming fans. Jazz is popular, and perhaps the best known Thai jazz composer is King Bhumibol Adulyadej, who plays both the saxophone and clarinet. The pop and classical violinist Vanessa-Mae is half-Thai and half-Chinese.

MUSICAL INSTRUMENTS

Princess Maha Chakri Sirindhorn plays several Thai classical musical instruments. She is an active leader in the movement to revive interest in the rich cultural value of Thai music among the younger generations.
(*A Closer Look, page 60*)

Below: These high school students play modern musical instruments in their school band.

Left: An artist puts the final touches on a Buddha statue. Artists must adhere to specific guidelines when creating the Buddha image. The artists who follow these guidelines with the most precision and beauty are chosen to create Buddha images for temples.

Painting, Sculpture, and Woodcarving

Traditionally, Thai paintings, sculptures, and woodcarvings were used to decorate temples or as parts of Buddhist religious teaching. Modern Thai artists continue the tradition of religious art but have also been influenced by Western artists.

Traditional religious paintings took the form of murals along temple walls. The murals depict stories from the *Ramakian*, the *Jataka Tales* (stories of the Buddha's life), or other stories dealing with Buddhist worship. The mural painters also included scenes from daily life. Buddhist monks used the paintings to teach others about Buddhism.

In the past, sculpture was usually limited to sculptures and carvings of statues of the Buddha, known as Buddha images. Some sculptures that still exist today date back to the sixth and seventh centuries, long before there was a Thai kingdom.

Woodcarvings decorated temples that were built as early as the Sukhothai kingdom. By the late 1700s, the art had already reached a high level of craftsmanship, and woodcarving was used to decorate not only temples but also palaces and homes. Woodcarving was commonly used to adorn the doors, windows, and roof and ceiling beams of Thai buildings.

Above: Decorative woodcarving designs are intricate and elaborate and include lotus flowers, guardian angels, giants, and dragon spirits.

Leisure and Festivals

Leisure

Thai people like to relax in the company of friends and family, and the unwritten rule is, "the more the merrier." Thai rarely go out in pairs. Instead, they prefer to be in larger groups that often consist of people of different ages.

The most popular times for relaxing with friends and family are on Saturday nights and Sundays. People who live in cities often go out to watch a movie or have dinner at a restaurant. Movies are imported primarily from the West and Hong Kong, although Thailand has a small movie industry. People living in the countryside often meet at a friend's house to play cards, watch television together, or just visit.

Teenagers like to go out together in groups usually made up of at least six people and often as many as twenty. One popular activity is going on picnics. Of course, this means bringing lots of food and at least one guitar, so friends can sing together. It is rare for young people to go out on dates as a couple. Only when

Above: **Sports and exercising are popular pastimes. Here, tai chi enthusiasts exercise in the cool of the morning. Tai chi is a Chinese exercise discipline with its roots in Taoism.**

Left: **Boys pose in front of movie posters promoting a Thai movie (*left*) and a Chinese movie (*right*).**

teenagers are older, perhaps after they have finished high school, will they start to have dates with a boyfriend or girlfriend.

Thai people still play traditional Thai games, as well as international sports, such as soccer and basketball.

Above: **These men are putting this elaborate and colorful kite together for a competition.**

Kite Flying

Kite flying is a traditional sport that began hundreds of years ago. Kites are flown throughout the year, but the competition season is from February to April, when the dry winds of the northeastern monsoon provide the strong winds needed for the large competition kites. Thai kites are made of bamboo and paper. A typical kite contest is between two teams. One team flies a large star-shaped kite called a *chula* (choo-lah). The other team flies several smaller, diamond-shaped kites called *pakpao* (park–pow). On the ground below, the field is divided so each team has its own area. Each team tries to make the kite from the other team fall into its own area. The chula team tries to tear the pakpao by using the sharp points of the star. The pakpao team tries to block the wind that is needed to keep the large chula aloft.

Takraw

Takraw (tah-kraw) is the name of a traditional Thai game that uses a small ball woven from rattan. There are three ways to play takraw: circle takraw, basket takraw, and net takraw. In all three games, players use their feet, knees, elbows, and heads to keep the ball in play. The use of hands is strictly forbidden. In circle takraw, the players stand in a big circle and try to keep the ball from hitting the ground, scoring points each time they keep the ball in play. In basket takraw, players try to put the ball through a ring in the middle of the court. Net takraw is played like volleyball — two teams try to score by knocking the ball down on the other team's side of the net.

International Sports

Soccer is the most popular international sport in Thailand. In Thailand, as in most parts of the world, the people call this game *football*, not soccer. Basketball is also increasingly popular. Thai television often broadcasts the National Basketball Association (NBA) games from the United States, so many Thai are fans of

Below: Takraw games are a common sight in public parks, wat compounds, or wherever there is a vacant plot of land. Shown here is a game of net takraw.

American teams. Badminton, volleyball, and tennis are favorite sports among young and old alike.

Kickboxing

Muay Thai (moo-ay tie), or Thai kickboxing, is a unique martial art form. It is a combination of boxing and tae kwon do. Most of the time, muay Thai kickboxers use their fists, but they may also use their feet, elbows, and knees. Each kickboxing match lasts for five three-minute rounds. Kickboxing matches are shown on Thai television every Sunday afternoon.

Animal Sports

Competitions involving animals are ancient pastimes that are still popular in rural areas. The most popular sport is cockfighting. There are also buffalo races and bullfights. Even small animals, such as beetles and fish, are trained to fight. Spectators often place bets on the outcome of a competition.

Above: **Thai kickboxers train for a match. Kickboxing is as popular in Thailand as soccer is in Europe.**

THE *RAMAKIAN*

Some kickboxing techniques are inspired by stories from the *Ramakian*. For example, one of the moves reenacts a scene in which the monkey king Hanuman leaps into the sky to break an enemy elephant's neck.

(A Closer Look, page 62)

Buddhist Festivals

Buddhist holidays are important days in the Thai calendar. They mark special events in the life of the Buddha. The most important Buddhist holiday is Wisaka Bucha, which takes place in late May or early June. Wisaka Bucha celebrates three important events in the Buddha's life: his birth, the day of enlightenment, and his death. *Khao Pansa* (kow pun-sah), or Buddhist Lent, is the time of year when Buddhists give extra attention to worship and prayer. During the Khao Pansa season, from July to October, Buddhist monks remain in the temple, studying the Buddha's teachings, meditating, and praying. Many Thai men and boys become Buddhist monks during this period.

Loy Krathong

Loy Krathong (loy krah-tohng) is celebrated on the first full moon after the rice harvest, usually in November. This ceremony began hundreds of years ago. It was a part of the celebration to thank the water spirits for all the water they provided during the growing season. The word *loy* means "to float," and the word *krathong* refers to a small raft. On the night of Loy Krathong, the rivers are full of rafts and colorful, candlelit banana-leaf bowls, floating under the moonlight.

Songkran

Songkran (sohng-krahn), or the Thai New Year, is celebrated from April 13 to April 15 throughout Thailand. It is the hottest time of the year. The word *songkran* comes from an ancient language called Sanskrit and refers to the beginning of a new solar year. On the eve of Songkran, people clean their houses and burn all their trash to begin the new year fresh and clean. During Songkran, Thai Buddhists visit temples to offer baskets of food and clothing to the monks.

Agricultural Festivals

Agricultural festivals are intended to ensure good harvests. In the Royal Plowing Ceremony in May, oxen plow a small area of the Royal Field to plant rice that has been blessed. The rice spirit is asked to bless the harvest. Another traditional planting festival is the Rocket Festival, celebrated in the northeast. Villagers try to call down the rains by firing rockets into the sky.

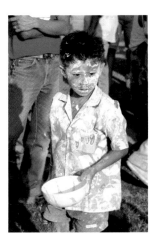

Above: **One popular activity during Songkran is splashing water on one another. Long ago, people believed that this practice would bring rain. Traditionally, people also sprinkled water on parents and grandparents as a sign of respect, but now children and adults go into the streets and pour bucketfuls of water on one another. People who do not want to get wet must stay indoors!**

Opposite: **Loy Krathong is celebrated everywhere in Thailand, and probably most spectacularly in Sukhothai. Shown here is a raft bearing a brilliant display of lanterns.**

Food

Mealtime

A common greeting, especially when welcoming a guest, is "Have you eaten yet?" Meals are important not only for eating but for socializing as well. Mealtimes give families and friends a chance to spend time together and relax.

Traditionally, Thai meals were served on the floor. Thai people would sit in a circle on a special straw mat, with the dishes served on a tray in the middle. Today, some people still eat this way in rural areas and at special traditional events, but, more often, people sit around tables for their meals.

FOOD ART

Thai dishes are often accompanied by fruit and vegetables that have been painstakingly carved to look like flower blossoms, boats, or other decorations.

Thai Flavor

Many Thai dishes combine sweet, sour, salty, and hot flavors for a unique taste found in no other type of cooking. Among the most popular Thai dishes are the many curries. A curry combines many spices with coconut cream, meat, and vegetables to make a thick sauce. Curries are sweet, sour, spicy, or a combination of all three.

Left: **Thai food takes a long time to prepare because it requires fresh ingredients that must be chopped, sliced, and ground. It may take two hours to prepare all the ingredients.**

Other popular foods are spicy coconut milk soups, grilled chicken and pork, or stir-fried vegetables. Rice is served with almost every meal. Noodles were borrowed from the Chinese, but Thai sauces make them unique.

Above: **Fast food, Thai style: this woman serves crispy pancakes from her paddle boat.**

Fruits and Desserts: Sweet and Colorful

Fruits and desserts are presented in colorful ways. Desserts include coconut custards and cakes made from rice flour and coconut cream.

A variety of fruit grows in Thailand. Throughout the year, there is always a fruit of some kind in season. Thai people almost never eat canned fruit. Thailand has all the common tropical fruits, such as coconuts, mangoes, papayas, pineapples, melons, and bananas. It also has regional fruits, such as rambutans and litchis. Thailand is famous for its durians. Durians have hard, spiky shells and yellow, creamy, rich meat. The ripe durian has a very strong smell. Because of this pungent smell, it is against the law to carry durians on buses or airplanes, or in hotels. Despite the strong smell, many people find the meat delicious and healthy, making durians the most expensive fruit in Thailand.

RICE

The most important food in the Thai diet is rice. Usually rice is served with other dishes of meat, fruit, and vegetables that are placed on top of the rice to add flavor.

(A Closer Look, page 66)

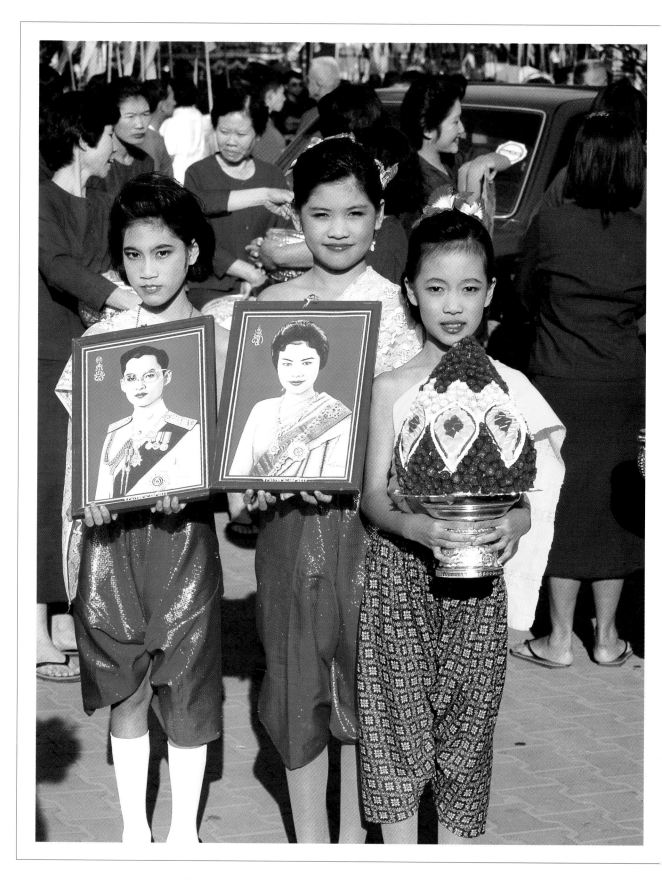

A CLOSER LOOK AT THAILAND

The Thai people are justifiably proud of their beautiful land and its history of freedom and cultural splendor. Watered by the famous Mekong and Chao Praya rivers, Thailand boasts some of the world's most luxuriant rain forests. In stark contrast to these serene natural treasures are bustling cities such as Bangkok, where life goes on at a hectic pace.

Despite the modernity of many Thai cities, strong ties to the past remain. Splendid monuments date back to the early kingdoms of Sukhothai and Ayutthaya, and traditional art forms, such as music, dance, and theater, keep alive the Thai heritage.

Opposite: **The birthdays of both the king and queen are public holidays celebrated with music and dance.**

Thai of all backgrounds and political persuasions are united by two longstanding institutions. Buddhism, the national religion of Thailand, dominates almost every facet of Thai life. Temples have been built throughout the country, Buddhist festivals are observed with enthusiasm, and Buddhist monks wield considerable influence in Thai society. Another shared passion is the Thai people's respect for their monarchy, from the achievements of King Mongkut to those of the current king, Bhumibol Adulyadej, the world's longest reigning monarch.

Above: **Chess is a game that almost every Thai knows how to play.**

43

Architecture

The traditional Thai house was built on stilts with a high open space and many windows to catch the tropical breezes. These houses used wooden pegs instead of nails to join the different pieces of wood together. This type of house is still found throughout the country, with some regional variations. One common style features steep roofs, decoratively carved moldings, and slightly inward-leaning walls. The shophouse is an urban version of the traditional Thai house. This is a two- or three-story building in which the first floor serves as a store or office, and the upper floors are the family residence.

Traditional Thai architecture declined around 1900, when buildings were increasingly built in European styles. The construction of old-style classic buildings has almost ceased, especially in the capital. From the late 1940s, European influence grew rapidly as local architects enthusiastically embraced the concepts of Western architects. Today, the skills of the traditional carpenters are all but lost.

Below: **The stilts on this Thai house raise it off the ground and protect the house from floods during the monsoon season. At night, the area under the house serves as a safe place to protect livestock. Today, this area is also used as a garage for tractors, motorcycles, and pickup trucks.**

Temple Architecture

Thai Buddhist architecture shows Chinese, Indian, and Cambodian influences, yet it has a distinctive style of its own. The roofs are high and gabled, often decorated with ceramic tiles in bright colors, such as orange or green. Building materials vary, especially among regions, and may include wood, plaster, and stone. As temples are the sites for meditation, the designs are open, usually with large windows and doors that allow breezes to flow through and keep the insides cool.

Classic temple decorations include magnificently carved wooden panels, which are used for gables, doors, and windows. These panels are often inlaid with splendid mother-of-pearl decorations. Glass mosaics and stucco embedded with multicolored pieces of porcelain are also classic decor. Temples may be adorned with gold leaf or similar material. This creates a glistening effect in the sunlight and a twinkling effect at night in the reflection of candles or lanterns. In many temples, the interior walls are painted with intricate, colorful murals that tell the story of the Buddha's life or with morality fables used in teaching Buddhist precepts.

Above: **The most spectacular Buddhist architecture can be seen at Wat Phra Keo, Temple of the Emerald Buddha, in the Grand Palace, Bangkok. The temple is guarded by colorful stone spirits, Chinese giants, bronze lions, and the mythical eagle-like garuda.**

45

Bangkok

Most visitors to Thailand are greeted first by the hustle and bustle of Bangkok, the capital and largest city. Bangkok is the cultural, political, and economic center of Thailand.

Bangkok has a population of over 11 million people, and this number continues to increase as more people from the rural areas come to Bangkok in search of work opportunities. The growth in population has resulted in congestion and overcrowded slum areas. Some sources estimate that roughly 1 million people live in slum conditions.

Bangkok used to be called "the Venice of the East" because its original buildings stood on stilts above the Chao Phraya River. A system of canals, on which people were ferried by boat taxis, crisscrossed the city. The canals also served as marketplaces, where merchants used small boats to peddle their goods throughout the city. As Bangkok grew larger, cars became more popular, and all

Below: **At night, Bangkok comes to life with bazaars, bars, and discotheques.**

but a few canals were filled and paved to make roads. However, one floating market still remains in Bangkok and is a popular tourist site. River taxis still carry passengers up and down the Chao Phraya River, which now runs through the heart of the city.

The increase in roads made by filling in the canals is still not enough to handle the increase in traffic that is accompanying the city's population growth. Some sources doubt that the metro train system, which commenced in 1999, will improve the congestion. Bangkok has some of the worst traffic jams in Asia, if not the world. Perhaps the longest one was in 1995 during the Songkran public holiday, when, at its worst, it took drivers fourteen hours just to leave the city.

Above: **Traffic police in Bangkok wear face masks because of the air pollution. Police stations are equipped with oxygen tanks in case exhaust fumes overwhelm the officers.**

Pollution

Another problem in Bangkok is pollution. All the vehicles in the streets of Bangkok contribute to air pollution. The Chao Phraya River is polluted by industrial waste from factories and household sewage that drain directly into the river. Although the Thai government is making efforts to clean up the environment, it is a challenging task.

Buddhism

Buddhism is the national religion in Thailand. Ninety-five percent of the Thai population is Buddhist.

Buddha: A Prince who Became a Teacher

The Buddha began his life as a prince named Siddhartha Gautama (563–483 B.C.), who lived 2,500 years ago in northern India. Siddhartha gave up all his riches to search for the meaning of life. He followed a life of poverty and meditation. One day, while meditating under a tree, he found the answers to his questions. This special event was called *enlightenment*. From that day on, people called him the *Buddha*, which means "he who

understands." The Buddha taught people to live simply and not pay too much attention to material things.

Buddhists believe that when people die, they are reborn, or reincarnated. People may be reborn as people or as animals. A person who lives a good life will probably be reborn as someone privileged, such as a prince; a person who has lived an evil life will be reborn as something bad, such as a worm. Buddhists earn merit by doing good works, serving monks, meditating, and helping others. Their goal is to attain enlightenment.

Above: **Young men undergo a purification rite when they become monks. In the past, all Thai young men, including the kings, became Buddhist monks for at least a short period of time before their twentieth birthdays. Today, fewer young men observe this practice.**

The Three Jewels

For Thai people, the most important aspects of Buddhism are known as the triratna, or three jewels. The triratna consist of the Buddha, his teachings, and the Buddhist monkhood. The Buddha is followed as a great teacher and not as a god, although some people worship him as if he were a deity.

Buddhist Monks

While the Buddha was alive, many people came to hear him speak about how to live. Before long, a group of students dedicated their lives to studying the teachings of the Buddha. They became Buddhist monks. They gave up all their possessions, shaved their heads, and pledged to follow a simple life of study and teaching. They wore robes and ate food donated by people

Below: **Every morning, monks awake early and walk through the neighborhood streets carrying large bowls. Residents place food in the bowls. Giving food to monks is one way for Buddhists to earn merit.**

who wanted to support them. After the Buddha died, these monks traveled and spread the teachings of Buddhism throughout Asia.

Despite their lives of poverty, monks are respected for their education and the wisdom they teach to common people. Even the king bows to monks. Buddhist monks occupy a special place in Thai life, and many Thai men become monks for short periods of time to seek better understanding of the teachings of the Buddha.

Deforestation

The forest products of Thailand have long been a resource prized around the world. The teak that grows in the forests of the north produces a hard wood that is resistant to rot and attack by insects. However, teak is increasingly difficult to find in Thailand because of years of timber harvesting without managing the forest as a renewable resource.

Throughout Thailand, deforestation has become a problem. In the early 1900s, nearly 80 percent of Thailand's total land area was covered with forests. Today, only 5 percent is covered by undisturbed forest. There are many reasons for the loss of forest land. Population growth has required that the forests be cleared for settlement and agriculture. Commercial logging has contributed to deforestation as well.

Deforestation has hurt the environment in many ways. The habitat of many wildlife species has been destroyed, and some animals face extinction as a result. Erosion and flooding occur

Below: **Illegal logging takes place along the Myanmar border. While there are laws for sustainable forest management, some loggers try to get around these laws.**

Above: **The tiger is a predator that requires large areas of forest in which to hunt for food.**

downstream from areas denuded of forests. In 1988, a landslide, believed to be a result of intensive logging, killed 300 people in a village in southern Thailand. Since then, there has been a total logging ban in Thailand, although illegal logging still occurs.

Another reason for the loss of forest land is the construction of dams. Dams are used to help control water for irrigation and also as a source of hydroelectric energy. In recent years, the construction of large dams has been questioned by environmental activists because dams change wildlife habitats and human living patterns. In a recent case, the Nam Choen Dam in western Thailand was part of a government project to help provide electricity for Bangkok. Building it would mean that key areas from two of Thailand's most important nature reserves would be submerged, thus shrinking the available wildlife habitat. In addition, many villages would be displaced. Community and environmental activists raised national and international awareness of these threats. After years of protest, the dam project was cancelled in 1989.

The Golden Triangle

The region that includes the northern tip of Thailand, the western tip of Laos, and the eastern corner of Myanmar is called the Golden Triangle. Its center is near the town of Chiang Rai, where borders from all three countries meet along the Mekong River. This area is notorious for the production and trafficking of opium and heroin, two illegal and very addictive narcotics.

Opium has been a part of trade in Thailand for hundreds of years. In the 1800s, Western merchants imported the drug, but today, the growing and selling of opium is illegal.

Opium is extracted from the opium poppy, a flower that is cultivated by hill tribe peoples in the mountainous regions of Thailand, Myanmar, and Laos. These farmers sell the opium paste to traders, who then sell the substance to illegal heroin production plants. Heroin is more addictive, more expensive, and more easily transported than opium paste. Heroin produced in Thailand is smuggled into the United States and Europe.

Below: **Women from the Akha tribe pick opium poppies. Although opium production has been illegal since 1959, opium is still grown in remote areas of Thailand.**

As early as the 1970s, Thai and U.S. law-enforcement agencies have worked together to end these activities. Specific steps include intercepting drug trafficking networks and prosecuting drug traders. The authorities also provide economic assistance to the hill tribe groups. Using crop substitution programs and technical assistance, the governments help the hill tribe farmers find other employment. These programs are succeeding in Thailand. Opium is still produced in Myanmar and Laos. Heroin refineries have moved to these countries, but the heroin is still transported through Thailand because it has better roads and communication systems.

Many tourists come to Chiang Rai to see the Golden Triangle and the opium poppies. The pleasant climate also appeals to people trying to get away from the heat of the central plain. The Thai government hopes to work with the governments of Laos and Myanmar to develop the region as a tourist center, so the locals can work in the tourist industry rather than in the illegal drug trade.

Above: **While Thailand no longer produces a significant amount of opium, it remains an important transfer point for heroin en route to international markets.**

Hill Tribes

Mountain Dwellers

The mountains of the northern region of Thailand are inhabited by groups of people known as hill tribes. Most of these peoples migrated to the region from Laos, Myanmar, or southern China over the last one hundred years. The six major hill tribe groups are the Akha, Lahu, Lisu, Karen, Hmong, and Yao.

Each group has its own language, customs, and traditions and can be distinguished by its traditional form of dress. The tribes live in different locations, and there is very little mixing among them. Although some hill tribe people have converted to Christianity or Buddhism, most have animistic beliefs. They believe that there are spirits all around them living in the forest, in the sky, and in the lakes and rivers. Hill tribe people offer prayers to the gods of the earth and sky to ask for a good rice harvest.

Below: **The helmet-like headgear worn by the women of the Akha tribe is adorned with silver balls, coins, and beads. The Akha are also known for the elaborate and colorful embroidery on their clothes.**

Mountain Agriculture

The hill tribe people plant a special kind of upland rice that grows on the mountainside. Unlike rice grown in the valleys of Thailand, upland rice does not require flooded fields. In addition to rice, the hill tribe people grow fruits and vegetables that they eat or sell in the market. After the rice harvest, many of the hill tribe people plant corn. For the meat in their diet, they raise pigs and chickens, or hunt wild game in the forest.

The hill tribe people practice swidden, or slash-and-burn, farming. They move to a new planting area every three to four years. To clear land for their crops, they cut down the trees in the forest and burn the logs and stumps. The ashes from the fire act as a fertilizer for the soil. When the soil is no longer fertile, the people move to another place and clear new fields. This form of agriculture worked well when the hill tribe population was small, but now that the population has grown, there is not enough land. The Thai government discourages this kind of agriculture and is trying to teach the hill tribe people modern farming methods that do not destroy the fertility of the soil, so the hills can be reforested.

Above: **Hill tribe children are never short of games to play. Here, two Akha boys amuse themselves with the feathers of a bird they caught.**

The King

As long as there has been a Thai nation, there has been a king. Until the early part of this century, Thailand was an absolute monarchy. The king was the spiritual head of the nation and responsible for laws, treaties, and government services. In 1932, the country became a constitutional monarchy, and the king lost his active role in running the government. However, as the spiritual and cultural leader of the Thai people, the king plays an important role in Thailand. He is also the protector of the Thai people and has the right to impose an immediate curfew or declare war on a foreign aggressor if he feels Thailand is threatened.

Although the king has no official political role, he can influence the government because of his support from the people. Thai people greatly respect and love the king, and therefore no Thai politician would ever go against the wishes of the king. For example, in 1973, when Thai soldiers attacked students who were protesting against the government, the king expressed his

Below: **A parade marks the king's birthday celebrations.**

Left: King Bhumibol Adulyadej, accompanied by Queen Sirikit, visits rural communities to listen to the problems of the villagers. He has initiated many programs to improve the lives of the Thai people. All the royal children participate in the king's projects.

KING MONGKUT

King Mongkut (Rama IV, r. 1851–1868) is best remembered for his role in Thailand's modernization. He was a Buddhist monk for twenty-seven years before becoming king at the age of forty-seven. As a monk, he studied Buddhism, politics, economics, and foreign languages. Thus, as king, he was well prepared to communicate with foreign dignitaries. Mongkut supported modern medicine and introduced new ship-building and military techniques to Thailand.

disapproval of the prime minister for allowing this to happen. The prime minister resigned because he knew that, without the support of the king, he would be unable to govern the country.

Although Thai people no longer have to bow and crawl in the king's presence, they are still required to show him great respect. Each time a movie is shown at Thai cinemas, the audience must stand while the king's anthem is played before the film. It is illegal to remain seated. Criticizing or being disrespectful to the royal family is also against the law. Five public holidays each year honor the royal family. Chakri Day (April 6) and Chulalongkorn Day (October 23) celebrate the Chakri dynasty and one of its most famous kings. The Queen's Birthday (August 12), the King's Birthday (December 5), and Coronation Day (May 5) honor the current king and queen.

King Bhumibol Adulyadej is the longest reigning king in Thai history, and is among the most loved by the Thai people. He is truly considered the people's king. He is known for his concern for his people's welfare and his work in improving their livelihood. He is active in supporting rural development programs, such as projects to improve the irrigation and drainage systems, cooperative farms, modern farming techniques, and the revival of traditional handicrafts as a source of income for rural people.

The Mekong River

The Mekong River begins in the forested mountains and uplands of southwestern China and flows 2,610 miles (4,199 km) to the South China Sea, passing through Myanmar, Laos, Thailand, and Cambodia. The river forms the border between Thailand and Laos. The river and its vast basin encompass complex and diverse ecosystems, including forests, paddy fields, tributaries, streams, and creeks. Farming and fishing in small communities remain the way of life for most people on the Mekong, and local livelihoods are closely linked to the forest systems and river flows. The Mekong is known throughout Thailand as the home of *plaa buk* (plah book), a giant plant-eating catfish that can reach 7 feet (2.1 m) in length and weigh up to 700 pounds (318 kilograms). Its meat and eggs are a local delicacy.

The Mekong along Thailand's northern border is a popular tourist site for rafting trips through the jungle. Most local activities and traditions — including rice cultivation, fish harvesting, boat races, and water festivals — are timed to the seasonal rise and fall of the Mekong.

For over 150 years, people have explored the Mekong for wealth and riches. In the 1830s, French explorers made an

Left: **Spanning the Mekong River, the Mekong Bridge connects Thailand to Laos.**

Above: **Villagers living in the river basin depend on the Mekong River for their supply of food.**

expedition up the Mekong in hopes that it would be a back route into the heart of China. Today, the river is seen as a potential basis for development of regional trade and industry. Thailand belongs to the Greater Mekong Sub-region, an economic and trade zone that includes southern China, Vietnam, Laos, Cambodia, and Thailand. This association plans to develop a road and transport network throughout the region and harness the hydroelectric potential of the Mekong. In 1994, Friendship Bridge, the first of several bridges planned, was constructed across the Mekong, between Thailand and Laos.

The damming of the Mekong for hydroelectric power generation is a controversial topic. While many recognize the benefits of electric power, there is concern for the environmental damage that the dams may cause. One of the tributaries to the Mekong was dammed in 1994. The local people claim that after the Pak Mun Dam was built, the quality and quantity of fish declined. This and similar cases are making the Thai government take a cautious look at building more dams along the Mekong.

Musical Instruments

Since ancient times, the Thai people have known how to make musical instruments and to adapt the musical patterns of other cultures to their own uses. In fact, there are several kinds of musical instruments which the Thai devised before they came in contact with the culture of India.

In all, there are about fifty types of Thai musical instruments. They can be divided into percussion instruments, bowed instruments, plucked instruments, and woodwinds. Some of the simpler percussion instruments were originally used as signaling or time-telling devices, before being added to the traditional orchestra. The first Thai musical instruments were given names according to the sounds they made: graw (small bamboo drum), grap (flat bamboo pieces clapped together), ching (cymbals), khawng (gong), and glawng (long wooden drum).

Later on, the Thai discovered more advanced methods of making musical instruments. For example, they took several grap and put them on a stand with the tones in order from low to high. This was the origin of the xylophone. There are also

Left: As Thai music evolved, the rules for combining instruments into ensembles were deliberately kept flexible. Instruments were combined to produce harmonious sounds that suited each particular performance or occasion.

stringed instruments, such as the saw, a simple violin-like instrument, and various woodwinds made from bamboo. While there are many ornate traditional Thai instruments, these are fancy variations of the original instruments made from bamboo, gourds, wood blocks, and other simple materials.

The classical orchestra is called a *piphat* (pee-paht), and consists of between five and twenty musicians. In the past, all Thai musicians were apprenticed to master musicians and learned to play and sing while performing. Now there are schools, such as the University of Fine Arts, that teach these skills.

In order to preserve Thai national music, modern Thai musicians are trying to devise a system in which Thai traditional music can be rendered into Western notation. The Music Association of Thailand, whose objectives are to promote Thai music and safeguard the welfare of musicians, is under royal patronage.

Above: **The Thai orchestra has its origins in the royal court during the Sukhothai era, as an ensemble of musicians accompanying classical dance and puppet theater.**

The *Ramakian*

The *Ramakian* is the most famous story in Thai literature and has influenced Thai everyday life for hundreds of years. Scenes from the *Ramakian* are painted on the walls of Buddhist temples; many Thai sayings have their origin in the *Ramakian*; and even some Thai kickboxing moves are named after events in the *Ramakian*.

The story of the *Ramakian* is actually the Thai version of the *Ramayana*, a poem first told in India 3,000 years ago. When Brahmin missionaries left India to travel to Southeast Asia, they brought the *Ramayana* with them. Brahmins worship the Hindu god Vishnu and believe that Rama is one of Vishnu's incarnations, or bodily forms. Soon, the *Ramayana* became popular wherever these missionaries traveled, and the story was changed little by little to include places and personalities from local cultures. For thousands of years, the story was passed from generation to generation by storytellers who memorized it and added new details and adventures.

Below: **Thai artists rendered buildings and costumes in a distinctively Thai style in this mural painting of an episode from the *Ramayana*.**

Although Thai authors had written Thai versions of the *Ramayana*, the first king of the Chakri dynasty (Rama I) wrote the official Thai version of the story, which is called the *Ramakian*. The story tells the life of Phra Ram, the king of the mythical city of Ayodhia. The most virtuous person in the world, Phra Ram always does what is noble and overcomes selfish emotions such as jealousy or greed. As prince, he allows his father to give the throne temporarily to his (Phra Ram's) brother and goes to live in the forest with his wife Seeda. While in the forest, Seeda is kidnapped by the evil demon Tothsakan. Phra Ram then sets off with the aid of his trusted friend Hanuman, a great monkey in charge of a monkey army. Phra Ram and Hanuman free Seeda from Tothsaka and his demons, after which Hanuman travels the world alone and experiences many adventures.

The influence of the *Ramakian* appears throughout Thailand. The name of the old Siamese capital Ayutthaya was taken from Phra Ram's kingdom Ayodhia. Many traditional dances, classical plays, and shadow puppet performances tell stories from the *Ramakian*. Since 1902, the epic has become part of Thailand's school curriculum, so all children are familiar with the characters and lessons from the tale.

Above: **A classical dance troupe in elaborate costumes reenacts episodes from the *Ramakian*.**

Refugees

From the mid-1970s to the mid-1990s, armed struggles between communist governments and anti-communist forces in neighboring Laos and Cambodia caused many Cambodians and Laotians to flee to Thailand for safety. Many Vietnamese refugees who landed in Thailand were known as "boat people" because they fled their own country in boats sailing across the Gulf of Thailand. For those fleeing communism, refugee camps in Thailand provided a temporary shelter. Thailand also became a coordinating center for the resettlement of refugees abroad. Thus many of those who went on to live in the United States, Australia, or Europe passed through Thailand first.

The refugee camps were mainly in the northeastern region, opposite Cambodia and Laos. After the fall of Soviet communism in 1989–1990, the Vietnamese, Laotian, and Cambodian governments became more open to cooperating with neighboring countries and providing a safe environment for refugees to return home. Cambodia, however, remains unstable, and the main

Below: **Many refugees, like this little girl, with the catch of the day and an optimistic spirit, hope for a better life elsewhere.**

Left: The conditions in refugee camps are difficult. Refugees are not free to go wherever they please but are restricted to a fenced compound. Conditions are often crowded, and there are no jobs for people. However, some camps provide children's education and promote the refugees' cultures.

political groups sometimes do battle, especially in areas near the Thai border. In 1997 and 1998, fighting in northwestern Cambodia sent groups of Cambodians fleeing into Thailand for temporary shelter. By 1999, most of these refugees had returned to Cambodia.

Refugees from Myanmar came in the mid-1980s, when the country was still officially named Burma. Most of these refugees belong to hill tribes, such as the Karen, who are seeking independence from Myanmar. In 1989, the military government crushed student protests, sending many students fleeing into Thailand. By the mid-1990s, over 100,000 refugees from Myanmar lived in up to thirty refugee camps along the Thai-Myanmar border.

The United Nations and the governments of other countries help the Thai government provide these refugees with assistance. Charity organizations also provide aid, particularly by linking refugees with family members who live in other countries and can provide homes for them.

Rice

Rice is undoubtedly the most important food in the Thai diet. When people ask one another if they have eaten yet, they often ask, "Have you eaten rice yet?" A meal without rice is not considered a proper meal. Much of the economy depends on rice, and rice farming still employs a large number of people. The agricultural calendar is based on the rice-planting cycle.

Rice Harvest

The main rice crop is planted after the rains come, marking the end of the hot or dry seasons and the beginning of the rainy season. The rice farmer soaks rice seeds from the previous harvest overnight before planting them in a nursery seedbed. The seedbed is a small area where the farmer grows the young rice shoots until they are big enough to transplant.

During the month that the young plants are growing in the seedbed, the farmer prepares the paddy field by plowing it. Traditionally, farmers used water buffalo to plow their fields, but now farmers use tractors or rotovators.

THAI RICE

Thai farmers grow many different types of rice. The most famous is called "jasmine rice" because of its strong, sweet fragrance.

Below: **The task of transplanting rice has to be done by hand.**

The rice is transplanted by hand in rows of small bunches. After planting the rice in the paddy fields, the farmer must watch the water level in the rice field. There must be a gradual flow of water, which covers the roots but does not drown the plants. In some areas, the farmers use irrigation water from lakes and dams so they have more control over the water supply. Other areas, however, depend on rainfall, and the farmer must hope for good weather. Too much or too little rain can ruin the entire crop.

The crop is ready for harvest about three months after planting. Farmers drain the fields if they are not already dry as the rainy season comes to an end. The rice is harvested by hand and then threshed to remove the rice kernels from the long stalks on which they grow. The rice is then dried and stored in a rice barn as the family's rice supply for the upcoming year. Any extra rice is sold in the market.

Above: **The people on this farm are threshing rice by hand. Until recently, farmers in one village would all help each other at planting and harvest time in a kind of trade. Now, however, it is common for farmers to hire helpers.**

Silk

A Part of Thai Culture

Thai people have been weaving silk for centuries. The wardrobe of every aristocratic Thai included numerous silk garments, rich with intricate gold embroidery. Ordinary people used silk for ceremonies and other special occasions. Thai silk is made with one color for the warp and another color for the weft. This gives Thai silk its natural sheen and luster and makes Thai silk unique in terms of color tones and blends. When a piece of Thai silk is held up to the light, the overall color tone changes with the angle of light.

Silkworms are raised primarily in the Khorat Plateau in the northeastern region. Silk production occurs in the northeast and around Chiang Mai in the northern region. Thailand faces serious competition from other countries, particularly China and Vietnam, where production costs are generally lower and quality is good. Moreover, as the Thai economy expands, the income that sericulture farmers earn is not keeping pace with the income that they can earn from many alternative occupations.

Above: **Some silk production centers in Thailand maintain their own mulberry gardens where they raise silkworms. These centers take charge of all aspects of silk production, from the cocoon-growing stage to the weaving of the finished product.**

Left: **Thailand has several large silk factories, but silk weaving remains basically a cottage industry, with thousands of households obtaining all or part of their incomes from it. Weavers often use hand-operated looms, and one weaver produces only about 4.4 yards (4 m) of silk cloth per day.**

The Silk Process

Raw silk is a natural product of the silkworm, a type of moth that feeds on mulberry leaves. Silk fiber comes from the cocoons of silkworms, which are raised in woven bamboo trays in a silk farmer's house or in a silk factory, or filature. A silkworm forms its cocoon by forcing two fine streams of thick liquid out of tiny openings in its head. The liquid dries and hardens into a cocoon consisting of a single thread, which is often as long as 547 yards (500 m).

At a filature, cocoons are sorted according to color, size, shape, and texture, as these factors affect the final quality of the silk. Then cocoons are placed in a vat of boiling water to separate the silk threads of the cocoons from the caterpillars inside. The silk filaments are unwound from the cocoons and combined to create threads of raw silk. These threads are then washed and bleached before undergoing a multistage dyeing process. Finally, the threads are wound onto drums and sent to weaving shops, where silk cloth is produced.

Above: **Thai silk is appreciated throughout the world for its beauty and elegance.**

Spirit Houses, Amulets, and Tattoos

Thai are generally superstitious and believe in astrology and fortune telling. Although most Thai are Buddhists, many still believe in the presence of spirits and magical powers that are not a part of Buddhism. Many Thai practice spirit worship or use magical amulets and charms to bring good luck or prevent evil.

Spirit Houses

In almost every Thai house, school, hotel, or business, there is a spirit house or spirit altar. The spirit house may be a simple little shelf high up in a corner, or it may be placed outside the house as a fancy, small-scale replica of a Buddhist temple. These are called *san phra phum* (sahn prah poom). Whatever their shape, their function is the same. These are the dwellings of the guardian house spirits. It is believed that these spirits can help the family in times of emergency or can make trouble if they are not appeased.

Below: **To keep the spirits satisfied, the house owners provide frequent offerings of fruit, flowers, incense, candles, clothes, and carved elephants.**

Left: A necklace can have several different amulets to give its wearer various kinds of protection or good luck. Both men and women wear amulets, although men commonly wear several amulets on a necklace, whereas a woman's necklace usually has just one amulet.

Amulets

Another practice intended to provide protection or good luck is the use of amulets worn as necklaces. The most common kinds of amulets, called *phra khruang* (prah krer-ang), are small images of the Buddha or famous Buddhist monks that bless and protect the wearer. Amulets made from animal parts, such as tiger teeth or elephant tusks, provide special protection against certain types of danger, such as snakebites. Other amulets contain special prayers or blessings to be recited during a time of crisis.

Tattoos

Tattoos are another way to ensure safety or good luck. Tattoo artists or Buddhist monks who are known to have special powers draw these tattoos. Tattoos get their powers from special designs or prayers said while the tattoo is being drawn. One kind of tattoo is believed to protect people from gunshot wounds; another kind is for strength. Tattoos are drawn on the upper body, usually on the back, chest, or arms. Many years ago, both men and women wore tattoos, but today these are usually worn only by men.

Below: Tattoos do not have to be seen to be powerful. Although most tattoos are drawn with blue or black ink, some are made with invisible ink!

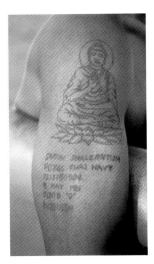

Tourism

Each year, around six million foreign tourists visit Thailand to enjoy the pleasant weather, beautiful scenery, and delicious food. Tourism is one of Thailand's biggest sources of income, and perhaps one reason why Thailand is well known around the world. Many tourists come on group tours, and younger tourists often travel alone or with friends. Tourism contributes approximately U.S. $6 billion to the Thai economy.

Perhaps the most memorable part of any visit to Thailand is the Thai people themselves. Their constant smiles and relaxed attitudes help tourists enjoy their stay. An important part of Thai culture is being a friendly and gracious host to guests. Thus, it is no surprise that tourists feel so welcome when they visit.

Because of the wide variety of cultures and landscapes within Thailand, there is an attraction for almost everyone in Thailand. Each region of Thailand has its own draws, and, throughout the year, there are always festivals to be enjoyed.

Below: **A popular tourist attraction in the north is mountain trekking, on foot or on ponies or elephants.**

Above: **The limestone formations of Phangnga, in southern Thailand, are a bizarre and beautiful sight.**

Bangkok and the central plain feature important historic sites such as the Royal Palace, the old capital at Ayutthaya, and the ancient ruins at Sukhothai. Beautiful Buddhist temples, streetside food stalls, the floating market, and other shopping venues are part of Bangkok's appeal.

The northern region is known for pleasant weather, beautiful mountain views, and hill tribe culture. The Songkran water festival each April is another big event that attracts tourists.

Tourists are also drawn to the easygoing, rural pace of northeast Thailand. This region features many influences from Laotian and Cambodian culture, which can be seen in the temples and artwork. This area is also the gateway to Laos and the place to see the famous Mekong River.

The south is known for islands that boast white sand beaches and clear blue oceans. The coral reefs and tropical fish draw tourists from around the world for snorkeling and scuba diving. The southern islands' dramatic limestone landscape appeals to many sightseers who enjoy exploring the cliffs and caves.

RELATIONS WITH NORTH AMERICA

Relations between North America and Thailand have generally been positive since they first began in the early nineteenth century. North America has consistently supported Thailand against threats to its independence, whether from European colonial powers or Asian communist countries.

Trade dominated nineteenth-century contact between Thailand and North America. Under King Mongkut, diplomatic ties strengthened, and by the end of the nineteenth century, representatives of Thailand and the United States had visited each other's country.

Opposite: **Phuket is a popular resort destination for North American and European vacationers.**

Above: **American flags are manufactured in Thailand.**

Relations continued to strengthen, especially after World War II. The United States provided financial and technical assistance for Thailand's agricultural programs. Thailand supported the United States by sending troops to fight in the Korean and Vietnam wars and sought security from its communist neighbors by becoming a staging area for U.S. troops.

Today, Thailand remains an important trade partner of North America. Thailand is considered one of North America's strongest political and economic allies in Southeast Asia.

Nineteenth Century: First Contacts

The first recorded contact between American traders and the Siamese king dates back to 1821, when the United States was only thirty-two years old, and twenty-eight years before Canada was given the right to self-governance. At this time, the United States was interested in trading with Siam for its natural resources, such as sugar, spices, wood, and tin.

In 1831, an envoy was sent by President Andrew Jackson to King Rama III. The Thai king responded by sending a number of gifts to the United States, including elephant ivory, tin, fine wood, incense, and pepper. The Commercial Treaty of 1833 was the first treaty between the two nations, and gave U.S. businessmen the right to conduct trade in Thailand.

Official relations between the two countries were limited until King Mongkut (Rama IV) took office in 1851. Before becoming king he had learned a lot from American missionaries, and was therefore pleased to increase friendly relations between the two countries. A second trade treaty was signed in 1856, and in the same year, the first official U.S. consulate was established in Bangkok.

Left: **President Andrew Jackson initiated the first official contact with Thailand in the nineteenth century.**

ENG AND CHANG: SIAMESE TWINS

The brothers who gave the world the term *Siamese twins* were born in 1811 in a village near Bangkok. Eng and Chang were joined at the chest and used this unique trait as the basis for their traveling show that played to audiences around the world. Despite their condition, the boys lived surprisingly normal lives, learning how to participate in many activities, such as swimming. At age seventeen, they left Thailand for the United States. In their act, they did acrobatics and horseback riding. They became wealthy and finally settled in the United States and became U.S. citizens. Each brother married, and between them they had twenty-two children. In 1873, Eng caught pneumonia and died. Chang died a few hours later.

Left: General William Sherman led the march through Georgia during the U.S. Civil War. A Thai citizen known as "Yod" fought with the Union Army during the war and participated in the march.

THE KING AND I

King Mongkut is the main character in the popular musical *The King and I*. It is based on the memoirs of Anna Leonowens, the royal children's English teacher. *The King and I* is banned in Thailand because of its historical inaccuracy and its disrespectful portrayal of King Mongkut. The king is depicted as immature and unable to deal with threats from foreign powers. Anna Leonowens was later found to have written false accounts of the king in order to sell more copies of her book. She, in fact, had very little direct access to the king. Many historians claim that King Mongkut was nothing like the character portrayed in the story. He was a brilliant statesman and an enlightened monarch, believed to be the first Asian ruler to speak, read, and write English fluently.

In the following years, King Mongkut exchanged letters and gifts with several U.S. presidents. In 1879, President Ulysses S. Grant visited Thailand as part of a world tour.

In 1862, a Thai citizen known as "Yod" volunteered to join the Union Army in the U.S. Civil War. He fought in the battles of Antietam and Gettysburg and joined in Sherman's march through Georgia. He was wounded on several occasions and was discharged after the war. He became a U.S. citizen in 1869 but eventually returned to Thailand.

The late 1800s brought further improvements in diplomatic relations between Thailand and Western countries. The first Thai consul to the United States was Isaac Smith, an American banker who was appointed by the Thai king to represent the Thai government. In 1884, the first Thai minister arrived in Washington, D.C., to meet with the U.S. president. The first member of the Thai royal family to visit the United States arrived in 1902.

Twentieth Century: Modern Nations, Modern Relations

The relationship between the United States and Thailand continued to strengthen in the twentieth century. In the early 1900s, an act of Congress gave Thai military cadets the chance to study in U.S. military academies. The practice of sending a limited number of Thai soldiers to study with the U.S. military still continues today. U.S. organizations, such as the Rockefeller Foundation, played a large part in supporting the development of medical facilities and planning within Thailand.

In 1941, the Thai prime minister formed an alliance with the Japanese, and in early 1942, the Thai government declared war on the United States and Britain. Seni Pramoj, the Thai ambassador to the United States, believed this declaration did not represent the real wishes of Thai citizens. He refused to deliver the official declaration of war to the U.S. government. Instead, he organized the Free Thai Movement with the goal of liberating Thailand from Japanese occupation. After the war, Thailand issued a proclamation that the declaration of war was void because it never represented the will of the people. The U.S. government accepted this proclamation, partly influenced by the Free Thai Movement and its cooperation during the war.

Above: **King Ananda Mahidol (r. 1935–1946), also known as Rama VIII, was the older brother of the current ruler, King Bhumibol Adulyadej.**

An Ally against Communism

Since World War II, Thailand has been an important friend to North America and its allies. In 1947, the United States opened an embassy in Bangkok, and in 1961, Canada established official diplomatic relations. Assistance from North America helped restore the war-torn country. Large aid programs in the 1950s and 1960s provided financial and technical assistance to improve the overall welfare of the Thai people. These programs included education, road and railway construction, agricultural and irrigation assistance, and rural health care improvement.

Military cooperation was a major part of Thai-North American relations after World War II. With communist China just above Thailand's northern border, both Thailand and the U.S. government feared that the Chinese would attack countries in Southeast Asia. In 1950, Thailand supported the United Nations force against communist North Korea by sending troops and supplies. In 1954, Thailand became the headquarters for the

A THAI PRINCE AT HARVARD

During the 1920s, Prince Mahidol Songkhla, the father of King Ananda Mahidol (Rama VIII) and King Bhumibol Adulyadej, studied medicine and public health at Harvard University in Boston, Massachusetts. The prince used this training to improve the standard of medical facilities in Thailand. King Bhumibol Adulyadej was born in Boston in 1927 and is the only monarch to be born on American soil.

Southeast Asia Treaty Organization (SEATO), which included the Philippines, the United States, France, the United Kingdom, Pakistan, Australia, and New Zealand. These countries pledged regional military protection if one of its members was attacked. SEATO disbanded in 1977.

Beginning in the early 1960s, military aid and cooperation from North America increased considerably. Thailand supported the United States in the Vietnam War, sending troops to fight with U.S. forces in Vietnam and providing military bases in Thailand for the U.S. soldiers to use. Today, Thailand and the United States conduct joint military training exercises.

Cultural relations also strengthened in the 1960s. King Bhumibol Adulyadej and Queen Sirikit visited North America in 1960 and 1967. U.S. President Lyndon Johnson visited Thailand in 1966; President Richard Nixon visited Thailand in 1969.

Below: **President and Mrs. Johnson extended a warm welcome to King Bhumibol Adulyadej and Queen Sirikit in 1967.**

Left: **President Bill Clinton's 1996 visit to Thailand was the first time in three decades that a U.S. president had visited Thailand.**

Present Relations

Throughout Thailand's economic growth during the 1980s and 1990s, North America was a strong ally. In the wake of the Thai economic collapse in 1997, the United States and Canada continued to show support for Thailand with monetary aid. However, the countries have not always agreed. For example, Thailand supported Myanmar's application to join ASEAN, but the United States opposed it, citing the Myanmar government's record of human rights abuses to its citizens as the reason. Despite occasional disagreements, relations between Thailand and North America have never been stronger. In 1996, President and Mrs. Clinton paid a visit to Thailand. Canadian Prime Minister Jean Chrétien visited Thailand in 1997.

Economic Ties

Trade relations between Thailand and North America continue to grow as part of the overall increase in trade activity in Southeast Asia. Thailand, Canada, and the United States are all members of the Asia Pacific Economic Cooperation (APEC), an organization of more than twenty nations from the Asia-Pacific region. APEC members work together to improve economic activity. Their goal is to remove all barriers to free trade by the year 2020.

The United States is one of Thailand's key trading partners, accounting for approximately 20 percent of Thailand's total exports. Major Thai exports to North America include computers and computer components, rubber products, seafood, and jewelry. The United States is the third largest importer of Thai products, behind Japan and the European Union. Thailand's top imports from the United States include semiconductors and aviation and office equipment.

Cultural Exchanges

Cultural exchanges between Thailand and the United States include student exchange programs at the high school and college levels. Usually students stay with host families to better understand the host country's culture and traditions.

Below: **American fast food is popular with young Thai, particularly those living in big cities such as Bangkok and Chiang Mai.**

Left: **World famous golfer Tiger Woods is the son of an American father and a Thai mother.**

Thai in North America

Over 300,000 Thai have settled in North America, with the largest communities along the west coast in cities such as Los Angeles, San Francisco, and Vancouver. Thai immigration to the United States accelerated during the period of close cooperation between the two governments in the 1960s and 1970s.

Thai immigrants usually blend in well with their American surroundings and rarely limit their friendships to only Thai or other Asians. Thai children born and raised in the United States speak English as a first language and many can only understand, but not speak, their parents' native language. To improve their skills, many Thai children attend Thai language classes.

About one-third of the Thai immigrants work in white-collar positions in medicine, banking, and other professions. The other two-thirds work in skilled or semi-skilled labor, often owning their own small businesses. Many Thai in the United States send money home to families that are still in Thailand. The chance for higher paying jobs in America is a strong draw for some poor Thai workers. Illegal immigration from Thailand does exist, usually in situations that exploit the illegal immigrant as a low-wage worker.

Above: **This Thai temple is in Los Angeles. There are over 150,000 Thai living in Los Angeles, which serves as a cultural center for Thai living in the United States.**

Buddhist Temples

There are over sixty Thai Buddhist temples in North America. The largest and oldest temple in the United States, Wat Thai Los Angeles, was established in 1967. These temples serve the social and cultural needs of Thai communities living in North America, and are often a focal point of life for Thai immigrants to North America. The temples usually offer classes in Thai language, culture, and Buddhism, as well as host Thai holiday celebrations. Non-Thai people are welcome, and these temples usually have American Buddhist participants who join in the temple activities.

Thai Food

The popularity of Thai food in North America has grown in recent decades. Thai restaurants are common in most large North American cities. In Los Angeles alone, there are over 400 Thai restaurants. Thai grocery stores are common in large metropolitan areas, and Thai cooking products, such as Thai curry powder, are often found in American grocery stores.

Below: **The distinctive flavor of Thai food has found a large following in the major North American cities.**

North Americans in Thailand

As early as the 1860s, the Thai government employed a number of foreign advisers in areas such as foreign affairs and financial and judicial reform. American doctors and engineers helped in the development of medical and transportation facilities within Thailand. American advisers in foreign relations were favored by the Thai government because the United States owned no colonies or territories near Thailand and thus was seen as politically neutral.

With the strengthening of diplomatic ties and increased economic aid to Thailand following World War II, the number of U.S. citizens in Thailand increased. As the Thai economy expanded, American companies established businesses in Thailand. Today, over 10,000 Americans live in Thailand. Thai are generally welcoming to foreigners. It is common for Thai people to invite Americans living in Thailand to join them in family outings and events.

Above: **Commuters wait to board the express boat on the Chao Phraya River in Bangkok. Most of the North Americans working in Thailand live in the capital city.**

Jim Thompson

The beautiful qualities of Thai silk were relatively unknown on the world market until after World War II, when an American named Jim Thompson saw the potential in the unique beauty of Thai silk cloth. He realized that, by improving the color quality, Thai silk could be sold around the world. Eventually, silk became Thailand's most famous luxury export. Many people think Thompson was single-handedly responsible for the success of Thailand's thriving silk export industry.

Thompson's love of beautiful things led him to decorate his residence in Bangkok with Thai artifacts, sculptures, paintings, and woodcarvings. His house has been left intact, and visitors today are able to share his appreciation of Thai art.

Thompson disappeared in 1967 while hiking in the hills of Malaysia. Today, his legacy lives on in a network of local retail outlets and worldwide distributors.

Below: **Jim Thompson's house in Bangkok is now a museum.**

A **B** **C** **D**

MYANMAR

● Chiang Rai

Taneh

Mae Hong Son ●

Chiang Mai ●

Nan ●

Wang

● Lampang

▲ Doi Inthanon
(8,514 ft/2,595 m)

Mekong

L A O S

1

Udon Thani ●

Ban Chiang ●

Phetchabun

Sukhothai ●

Phitsanulok ●

Ping

Yom

Mukdahan ●

Lam Pao Reservoir

Khorat Plateau

Chi

Nakhon Sawan ●

Nakhon
Ratchasima ●

Mun

Ubon
Ratchathani ●

● Surin

2

Chao Phraya

Khwae Noi (Kwai)

Ayutthaya ●

Thon Buri

Phanom Dangrek

Kanchanaburi ●

■ **BANGKOK**

● Samut Songkhram

Bilauktaung

Phet Buri ●

● Pattaya

Chanthaburi ●

CAMBODIA

3

*Andaman
Sea*

**Gulf
of
Thailand**

N

↑

*Isthmus
of Kra*

Ranong ●

4

Surat Thani ●

Phangnga ●

● Nakhon Si Thammarat

Thalang ●

● Krabi

Phuket ●

Phuket

Phi Phi

Malay Peninsula

Thale Luang

Songkhla ●

Hat Yai ● ● Pattani

5

*Gulf
of Tonki*

*South
China
Sea*

V I E T N

THAILAND

Above: The skyline of Bangkok is dominated by skyscrapers.

Andaman Sea A2–B5
Ayutthaya B3

Ban Chiang C2
Bangkok B3
Bilauktaung
    Mountains B2

Cambodia C3–D3
Chanthaburi B3
Chao Phraya River
    B2–B3
Chi River C2
Chiang Mai A1
Chiang Rai B1

Doi Inthanon A1

Gulf of Thailand B3–C5
Gulf of Tonkin D1–D2

Hat Yai B5

Isthmus of Kra A4–B4

Kanchanaburi B3
Khorat Plateau C2
Khwae Noi (Kwai)
    River A2–B3
Krabi A5

Lam Pao Reservoir C2
Lampang B1
Laos B1–D3

Mae Hong Son A1
Malay Peninsula B5
Mekong River B1–D4
Mukdahan C2
Mun River B2–C2
Myanmar A1–B4

Nakhon Ratchasima B2
Nakhon Sawan B2
Nakhon Si
    Thammarat B5
Nan B1
Nan River B1–B2

Pattani B5
Pattaya B3
Phangnga A4
Phanom Dangrek
    Mountains B3–C3
Phet Buri B3
Phetchabun
    Mountains B1–B2
Phi Phi (islands) A5
Phitsanulok B2
Phuket (city) A5

Phuket (island) A5
Ping River A1–B2

Ranong A4

Samut Songkhram B3
Songkhla B5
South China Sea D4–D5
Sukhothai B2
Surat Thani B4
Surin C2

Tanen Mountains A1–B1

Thalang A5
Thale Luang B5
Thon Buri B3

Ubon Ratchathani C2
Udon Thani C2

Vietnam C1–D4

Wang River B1–B2

Yom River B1–B2

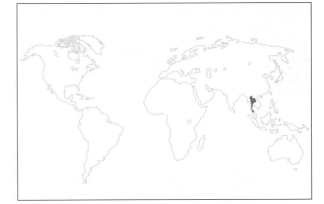

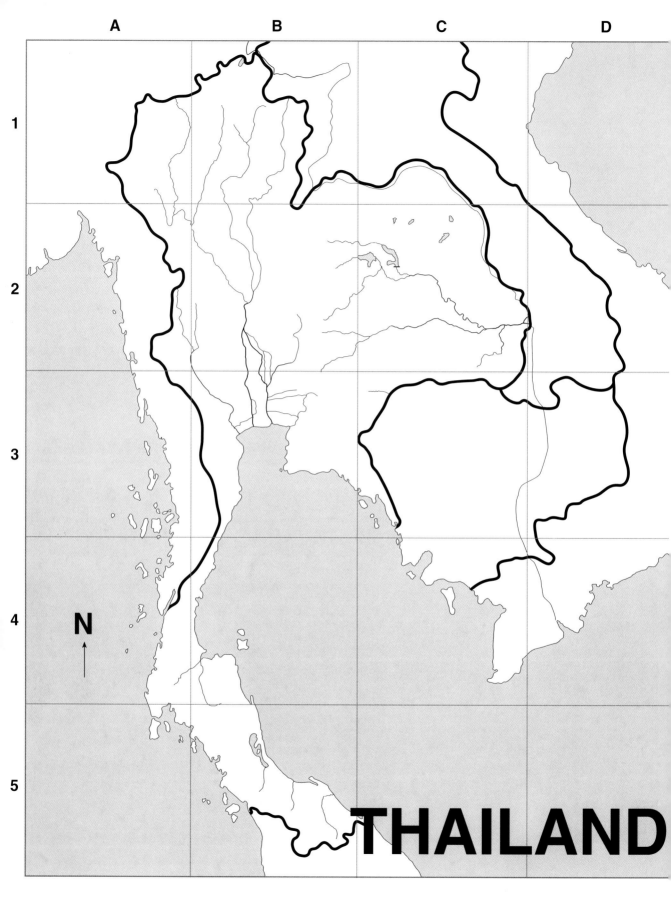

How Is Your Geography?

Learning to identify the main geographical areas and points of a country can be challenging. Although it may seem difficult at first to memorize the locations and spellings of major cities or the names of mountain ranges, rivers, deserts, lakes, and other prominent physical features, the end result of this effort can be very rewarding. Places you previously did not know existed will suddenly come to life when referred to in world news, whether in newspapers, television reports, or other books and reference sources. This knowledge will make you feel a bit closer to the rest of the world, with its fascinating variety of cultures and physical geography.

Used in a classroom setting, the instructor can make duplicates of this map using a copy machine. (PLEASE DO NOT WRITE IN THIS BOOK!) Students can then fill in any requested information on their individual map copies. Used one-on-one, the student can also make copies of the map on a copy machine and use them as a study tool. The student can practice identifying place names and geographical features on his or her own.

Above: **The landscape of Mae Hong Son in northwest Thailand is mountainous and densely forested.**

Thailand at a Glance

Official Name	Thailand
Capital	Bangkok
Official Language	Thai
Population	60,609,046 (1999 estimate)
Land Area	198,115 square miles (513,118 square km)
Provinces	Amnat Charoen, Ang Thong, Buriram, Chachoengsao, Chai Nat, Chaiyaphum, Chanthaburi, Chiang Mai, Chiang Rai, Chon Buri, Chumphon, Kalasin, Kamphaeng Phet, Kanchanaburi, Khon Kaen, Krabi, Krung Thep Mahanakhon (Bangkok), Lampang, Lamphun, Loei, Lop Buri, Mae Hong Son, Maha Sarakham, Mukdahan, Nakhon Nayok, Nakhon Pathom, Nakhon Phanom, Nakhon Ratchasima, Nakhon Sawan, Nakhon Si Thammarat, Nan, Narathiwat, Nong Bua Lamphu, Nong Khai, Nonthaburi, Pathum Thani, Pattani, Phangnga, Phatthalung, Phayao, Phetchabun, Phetchaburi, Phichit, Phitsanulok, Phra Nakhon Si Ayutthaya, Phrae, Phuket, Prachin Buri, Prachuap Khiri Khan, Ranong, Ratchaburi, Rayong, Roi Et, Sa Kaeo, Sakon Nakhon, Samut Prakan, Samut Sakhon, Samut Songkhram, Sara Buri, Satun, Sing Buri, Sisaket, Songkhla, Sukhothai, Suphan Buri, Surat Thani, Surin, Tak, Trang, Trat, Ubon Ratchathani, Udon Thani, Uthai Thani, Uttaradit, Yala, Yasothon
Highest Point	Doi Inthanon 8,514 feet (2,595 m)
Major Rivers	Chao Phraya, Mekong
Main Religion	Buddhism (95 percent)
National Symbol	The garuda, a half-human, half-bird figure from Indian mythology
Ethnic Groups	Thai 75%, Chinese 14%, Others 11%
Currency	Baht (37.8 Baht = U.S. $1 as of 2000)

Opposite: **A boy dressed in Shan costume takes part in the Handicraft Festival in Chiang Mai, Thailand.**

Glossary

Thai Vocabulary

ampoe (alm-per): an administrative district.

baht (bart): the Thai currency.

Chakri (chuk-kree): the name of the currently ruling Thai dynasty.

changwat (chang-watt): a political and administrative province.

chula (choo-lah): a kind of Thai kite that looks like a star.

Khao Pansa (kow pun-sah): an annual period of extra prayer and meditation observed by Buddhists.

khlong (klong): a canal.

khon (kohn): Thai classical theater that evolved from performances for royalty.

krathong (krah-tohng): a small, floating, candlelit raft.

lakhon (lah-kon): Thai classical theater for common people.

likay (lee-kay): traditional folk theater.

Loy Krathong (loy krah-tohng): a holiday honoring water spirits.

muay Thai (moo-ay tie): Thai kickboxing.

nang talung (nang tah-loong): a traditional shadow puppet theater performance.

nang yai (nang yeye): a traditional shadow puppet theater performance.

pakpao (park-pow): a kind of small, diamond-shaped Thai kite.

phra khruang (prah krer-ang): an amulet bearing either an engraving of the Buddha or an inscription by Buddhist monks.

Phrathet Thai (prah-tet tie): Land of the Free.

piphat (pee-paht): Thai classical orchestra.

plaa buk (plah book): a giant catfish found in the Mekong River.

Ramakian (rah-mah-kee-un): a famous Thai epic poem about good and evil. The *Ramakian* is based on the *Ramayana*, a classical Indian epic.

san phra phum (sahn prah poom): a small house for worshiping spirits.

Songkran (sohng-krahn): a festival welcoming the new year.

takraw (tah-kraw): a sport played with a ball made from woven cane.

wai (why): a polite, respectful bow.

wat (waht): a temple.

Wisaka Bucha (wee-sah-kah boo-chah): a Buddhist holiday celebrating the life of the Buddha.

English Vocabulary

animism: the belief that all natural objects, animals, and plants have souls.

archaeological: relating to the study of buried remains from ancient times, such as houses, pots, tools, and weapons.

colony: a country or area under the control of another country.

constitution: the system of laws and principles governing a country.

copra: the dried flesh of the coconut, from which oil is pressed for making soap.

coup: an unexpected overthrow of the government in power.

curfew: a regulation imposing the withdrawal of people from and the closure of businesses in a certain area at a stated time.

dialect: a regional variety of a language.

downturn: a downward trend.

durian: a spiky, pungent-smelling fruit.

dynasty: a line of rulers belonging to the same family.

ecosystem: an ecological system that relates all the plants, animals, and people in an area to their surroundings.

enlightenment: the state of having true understanding.

envoy: a messenger sent by one government to do business with another government.

excavation: the act of digging.

extinct: no longer existing.

extol: to praise highly.

filature: a factory where silk is drawn from silkworm cocoons.

gable: the three-cornered, upper end of a wall where it meets the roof.

garuda: a half-human, half-bird figure from Indian mythology.

habitat: the natural home of a plant or animal.

irrigation: a system of human-made streams or canals that supplies water to dry land.

litchi: a fruit with a hard, scaly outer covering and sweet, edible flesh.

mangrove: a type of tropical tree that grows on muddy land and near water and puts down new roots from its branches.

monsoons: strong seasonal winds.

monument: a building erected in memory of a great person or event.

mortar: a type of heavy gun with a short barrel, firing an explosive that falls from a great height.

mosque: a place of worship for Muslims.

mural: a wall painting.

nationalism: the pride people have in their nation.

philosophy: a set of rules or beliefs governing one's view of life and of the universe.

precepts: guiding rules.

rain forest: a tropical forest with an annual rainfall of at least 100 inches (254 centimeters).

rambutan: a fruit with a bright red, spiny outer covering and sweet, edible flesh.

rattan: a tropical plant with a strong stem that is easily bent and commonly used for making baskets and furniture.

refugee: a person who has been driven from his or her country for political reasons or during a war.

sanctuary: a place for birds and animals where they may not be hunted and their enemies are controlled.

sericulture: the production of raw silk by breeding silkworms.

swidden: land cleared for farming by burning away vegetation.

tapioca: a starchy substance prepared from the root of the cassava plant.

triratna: the three most important aspects of Buddhism: the Buddha, his teachings, and Buddhist monkhood.

undulating: having a wavy form or surface.

warp: threads running along the length of a woven cloth.

water buffalo: large black cattle with long, curved horns.

watershed: the region or area drained by a river or stream.

weft: threads running across the width of a woven cloth.

More Books to Read

Bangkok. Cities of the World (New York, N.Y.) series. Sylvia McNair (Children's Press)

Breath of the Dragon. Gail Giles (Clarion Books)

The Food of Thailand: Authentic Recipes from the Golden Kingdom. Food of series.
Sven Krauss and Wendy Hutton (Charles E. Tuttle)

The Land of Smiles and Royal White Elephants: Let's Travel to Thailand Together.
Jeannette P. Windham (Global Age)

Rice Without Rain. Minfong Ho (Lothrop Lee & Shepard)

A Tale of Two Rice Birds: A Folktale from Thailand. Clare Hodgson Meeker
(Sasquatch Books)

Thailand. Countries of the World series. Kristin Thoennes (Bridgestone Books)

Thailand. Enchantment of the World second series. Sylvia McNair (Children's Press)

Thailand. Festivals of the World. Harlinah Whyte (Gareth Stevens)

Thailand. Major World Nations series. Frances Wilkins (Chelsea House)

Thailand: Land of Smiles. Discovering Our Heritage series. Karen Schwabach (Dillon)

Traditional Festivals in Thailand. Images of Asia series. Ruth Gerson
(Oxford University Press)

Wild Thailand. Gerald Cubitt, Belinda Stewart-Cox, and John Hoskin (MIT Press)

Videos

Thailand — Land of 1000 Temples. (Education 2000)

Windows to the World: Thailand. (IVN Entertainment)

Web Sites

bangkok.com

www.geocities.com/Heartland/5226/thailand.html

www.wwfthai.ait.ac.th

Due to the dynamic nature of the Internet, some web sites stay current longer than
others. To find additional web sites, use a reliable search engine with one or more of the
following keywords to help you locate information on Thailand: *Ayutthaya, Bhumibol
Adulyadej, Chao Phraya, elephants, Golden Triangle, Mekong, Siam,* and *Sukhothai.*

Index *(Note: Thai names are alphabetized according to how they appear in the text.)*